Speaking of CLAY

A Vocabulary Resource for Ceramics Teachers and Students

by
Tracy Fortune

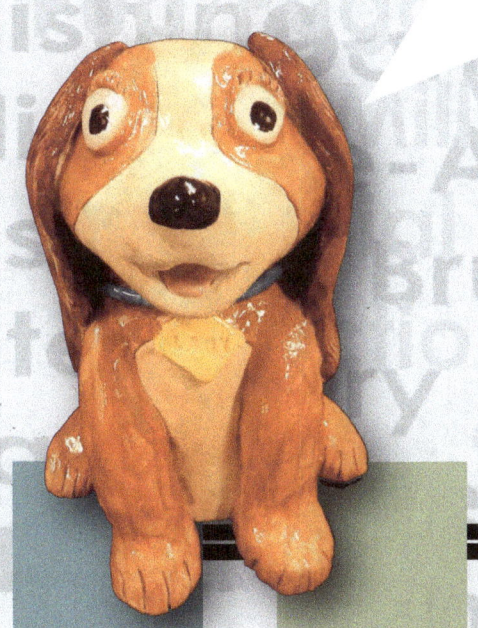

SPEAKING OF CLAY

A Vocabulary Resource for Ceramics Teachers and Students

By Tracy Fortune

National Board Certified Art Teacher

Bachelor of Education, Masters of Education

First Edition

Copyright © Tracy Fortune 2021

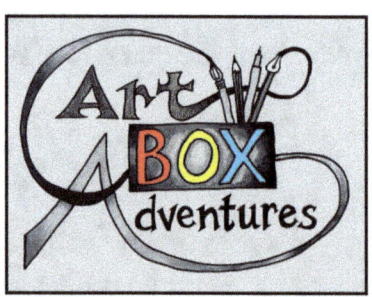

artboxadventures@gmail.com

www.artboxadventures.net

Speaking of Clay
Table of Contents

Introduction 4

Chapter 1: Attributes of Clay and Glaze..........................7

Chapter 2: Clay Tools and Equipment............................18

Chapter 3: Clay Methods Vocabulary 39

Chapter 4: Sculptural and Functional Clay Terms...............53

Chapter 5: Elements & Principles of Ceramic Design...........61

Chapter 6: Ceramic Studio Tips......................................81

Chapter 7: Glossary of Ceramic Terms..........................87

Content Index...98

Introduction

This book focuses on ceramics vocabulary and is designed as a resource for art/ceramics teachers and their students. There are many student-friendly pages that focus on key ceramics terms and concepts. Other pages are more in-depth and are suitable for ceramics teachers or advanced students who want to expand their knowledge.

This book is organized into chapters, each one focusing on the vocabulary terms relating to different aspects of ceramics including Tools & Equipment, Attributes of Clay & Glaze, Clay Forming Methods, and the Elements and Principles of Design. There is also a nine-page glossary of ceramic terms.

Other Books In the "All About Clay Series"

This book is one of the books in the All About Clay Series which are available in paperback from Amazon and as digital downloads.

1. Clay Inspirations: 125 Technique Based Challenges to Spark Your Imagination
2. Functional Clay Inspirations: 100 Functional Ceramic Challenges to Spark Your Imagination
3. Sculptural Clay Inspirations: 100s of Ceramic Artwork Ideas Organized by Theme/Subject
4. The All About Clay Student Handbook with Chapter Review Questions and Activities
5. "Speaking of Clay: A Vocabulary Resource for Ceramics Teachers and Students"
6. "Clay Matters: A Go-To Guide for Ceramics Teachers and Students"

I have taught art and ceramics for over 30 years in the United States, Canada, and Liberia, West Africa. I am a life-long learner and constantly on the lookout for resources to help me with my teaching. When I can't find what I am searching for, I often create the resources myself. This book is a collection of resources I have developed and am excited to share with you.

I hope this resource inspires you and your students.

Creatively,
Tracy Fortune
artboxadventures@gmail.com

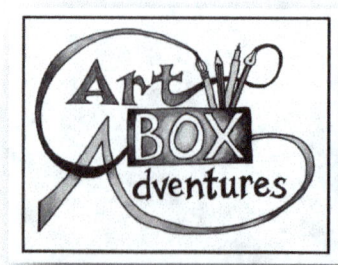

The 'All About Clay' Series

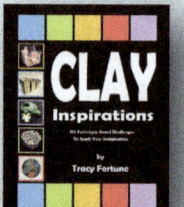
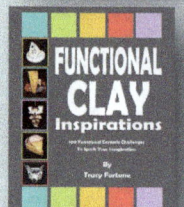
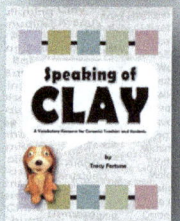
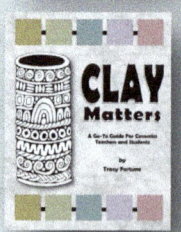
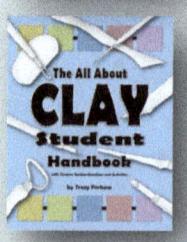
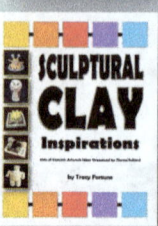

Introduction

How do you say 'Clay'?

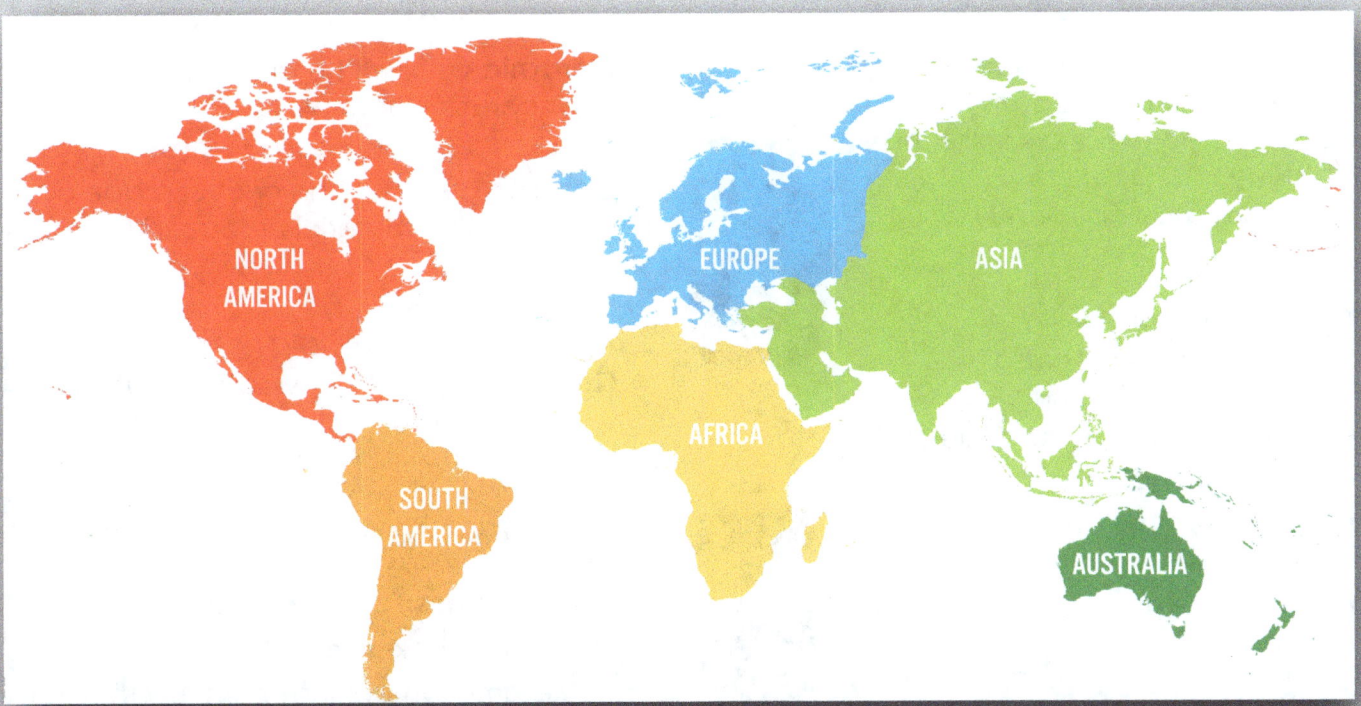

It can be said many ways....

Afrikaans: Klei
Among: Av Nplaum
Arabic: ﺻَﻠْﺼﺎل
Chinese: 粘土
English: Clay
Croatian: Glina
Czech: Hlína Hrnčířská
Danish: Ler
Dutch: Klei
Filpino: Luwad
Finnish: Savi

French: Argile
Gaelic: Crèadh
German: Lehm
Greek: πηλός
Hebrew: חימר
Italian: Argilla
Japanese: 粘土
Korean: 점토
Napali: माटो
Norwegian: Leire
Polish: Glina Skała

Portuguese: Argila
Romanian: Lut
Russian: глина
Samoan: Omea
Somali: Dhoobo
Spanish: Arcilla
Swedish: Lera
Thai: ดินเหนียว
Turkish: Kil
Ukrainian: глина
Vietnamese: đất sét

Comparing Terms: Clay, Ceramics & Pottery

Clay

Clay (noun) an earthy material that is plastic when moist, but hard when fired and used to make brick, tile, and pottery.

"That ceramic jug was made with red clay"

History of the Term Clay

From the Old English "clæg" meaning "stiff, sticky earth."

- Germanic *klaijaz and "Kleie
- Old Frisian klai
- Old Saxon klei
- Dutch clei
- Danish klæg

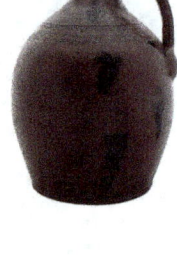

Ceramics

Ceramics (noun) the art of making and decorating pottery.

"I am taking a ceramics class"

Ceramic(s) (noun) an artifact made of hard brittle material produced from non-metallic minerals (clay) fired at high temperatures.

"There are ceramics on the table"

Ceramic (adjective) Made of material produced by the high temperature firing of inorganic, non-metallic rocks and minerals.

"A ceramic jug stood on the table"

History of the Term Ceramics

From the Greek word

- *"keramos"* meaning *"burnt earth."*
- *"keramic,* meaning "of or belonging to pottery."

Pottery

Pottery (noun)

- Objects (containers) that are made out of clay by hand.
  "The artist created beautiful pottery"
- A studio where pottery is made.
  "The artist worked every day at the pottery""

Pottery (adverb)

- the skill of making pots and dishes from clay.
  "The student took pottery class"

History of Term Pottery

- Pottery derived from the Old English term *"potian"* meaning "to push".
- A pottery (potter's workshop) comes from the Old French word *"poterie."*

What is the Difference Between Clay, Ceramics and Pottery?

Clay is a material that when fired becomes ceramic.

Ceramics are products such as bricks, stoneware, china, and tiles that are made from firing glass, cements, or clay.

Pottery is generally considered to be containers made from clay.

Attributes of Clay & Glaze

What is Clay? What is Glaze? Types, Properties, Stages & Sources

Chapter 1: Attributes of Clay

What is Clay?

Clay is...
a product from the earth that when heated becomes hard.

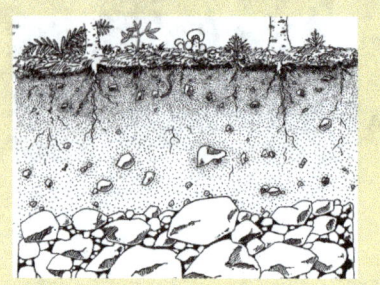

Geologically
Geologically, clay comes from decomposed igneous rock that has been eroded by weather. Clay is found near the earth's surface, often by rivers and lakes.

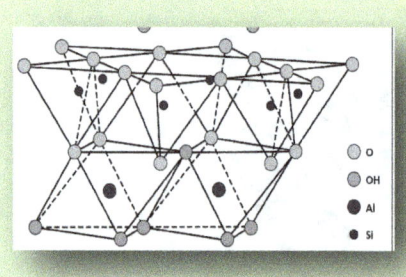

Chemically
Chemically, clay is a mixture of alumina, silica and water and has the formula

$$Al_2O_3 + 2SiO_2 + 2H_2O$$

Other mineral oxides and organic matter are also found in clays.

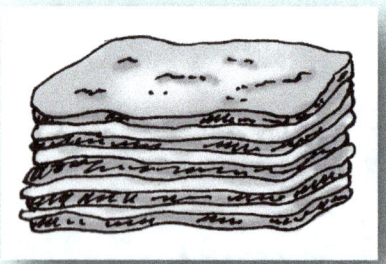

Physically
Physically, clay is plastic due to its thin plate-like particles and water content. It becomes hard and brittle with drying or firing. Clays naturally vary in color from white to dull grey, brown to orange-red.

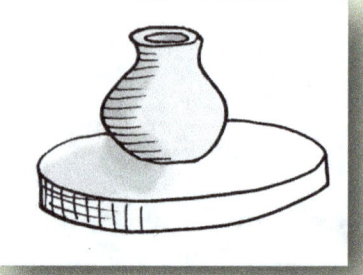

Artistically
Artistically, clay is an art medium that can be used to create both functional and sculptural items. Products can be handcrafted or mass-produced.

Chapter 1: Attributes of Clay

Types of Clay

Maturation Firing Temperture

- 2200–2600 — Cone 10 or higher
- 2150–2400 — Cone 4–10
- 1700–2000 — Cone 06–1

Porcelain
Very High-Fire Clay
(Cone 10 or Higher)
Known for strength, durability, whiteness, smoothness and transparency
Color: White

Stoneware
Mid-Fire Clay   &   High-Fire Clay
(Cone 4-7)   (Cone 8-10)
Has stone-like characteristics when fired making it strong, hard, durable and non-porous
Colors: White, buff, light/medium grey, brown

Earthenware
Low-Fire Clay
(Cone 06-1)
Course, opaque, easily workable clay that is still porous when fired
Colors: Red, orange, brown, white, buff

Chapter 1: Attributes of Clay

Sources of Clay

Clays and clay minerals are found mainly on or near the earth's surface.

Clay Cycle

When hot magma from under the earth's crust cools, it becomes a solid called igneous rock. Through weathering, this igneous rock is broken down from boulders to rocks, rocks to pebbles, and finally pebbles to small particles called platelets. These platelets are mixed with organic matter and clay is formed. Erosion carries sediment away from the original site of the igneous rock.

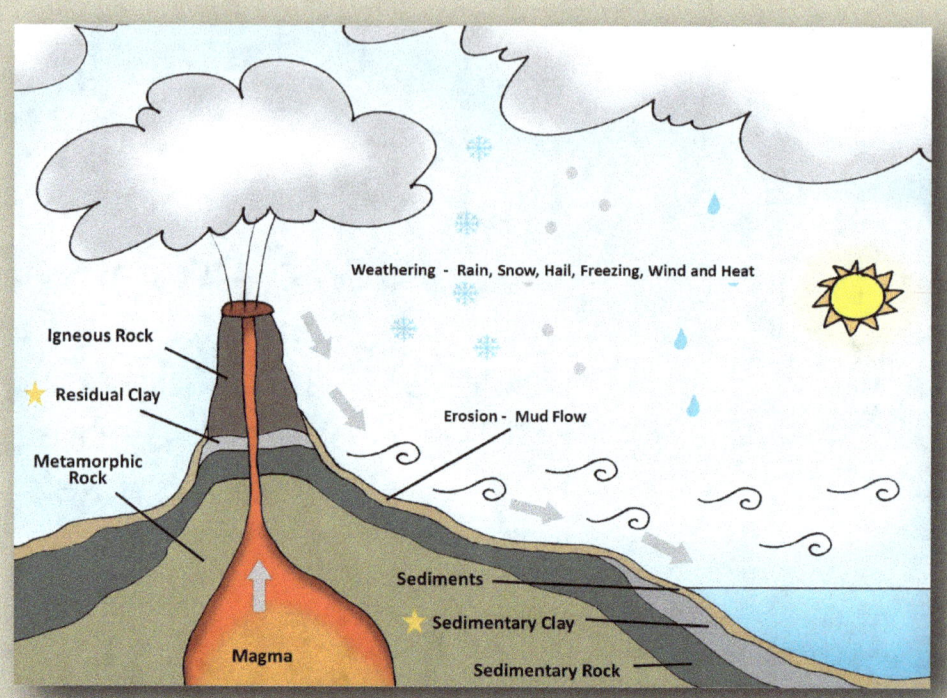

Primary Clay is found near the igneous (mother) rock and Secondary Clay is found away from the original site.

Two Classifications of Clay
Based on Where Clay Is Found

Primary (Residual) Clay resides at or near the original site where the igneous rocks were formed. It is the purest type of clay and has few or no impurities.
- **Names:** Kaolin, Porcelain, China Clay
- **Color:** White
- **Cone:** Δ10-12
- **Uses:** Industrial, Commercial, Residential Artists/Potters
- **History:** Used in China during the Eastern Han Dynasty (206BC–220 AD) and Tang Dynasty (618–907 AD). Porcelain production was introduced in Europe around 1720.

Secondary (Sedimentary) Clay has been broken down and moved from its original location by weathering and erosion to a new (sedimentary) deposit. Clay can accumulate minerals along the way and is often found near rivers, streams and lakes.
- **Names:** Stoneware, Earthenware, Ball Clay
- **Color:** Buff, Red, Brown, Grey
- **Cone:** Δ022-10
- **Uses:** Residential Artists/Potters
- **History:** Used in pre-historic times and common around the world

Properties of Clay

Color
The color of clay is determined by the presence and type of minerals in it.
Examples: Iron=Red/Brown, Manganese=Black/Grey

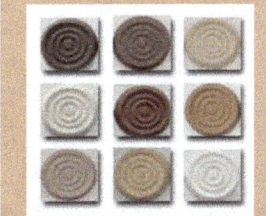

Plasticity (Workability)
Ability and ease of a clay body to be formed and molded.

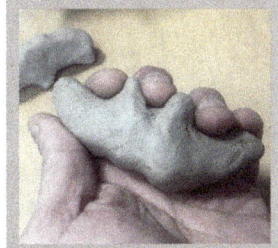

Texture (Smoothness)
The roughness or smoothness of clays can vary. Ones containing grog are rougher.
Grog: a granular material made from crushed, fired clay.

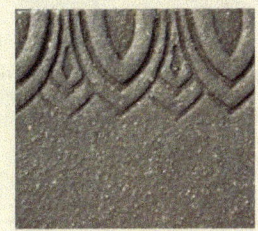

Maturation Temperature (Cone)
Temperature/Cone at which a clay matures/vitrifies and becomes its hardest and least porous.

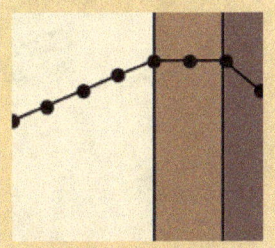

Porosity (Moisture)
The ability of clay to hold/absorb moisture.
Low fire clays are more porous.
Mid and high-fire clays are less porous.

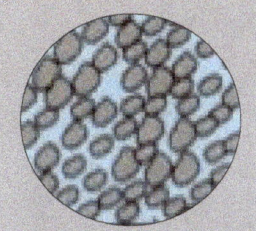

Shrinkage
The amount clay shrinks as it dries and after it has been fired. This can be up to 20%.

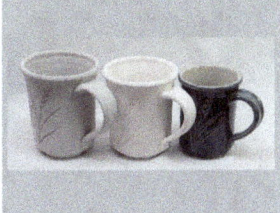

Chapter 1: Attributes of Clay

Clay Chemistry

What are the Main Components of Clay?

Potters are most interested in the periodic table elements that are found in the earth's crust. These elements, found in rocks, are present in clay and glazes. The most abundant elements are oxygen, silicon and aluminum, followed by iron, calcium, sodium, potassium and magnesium.

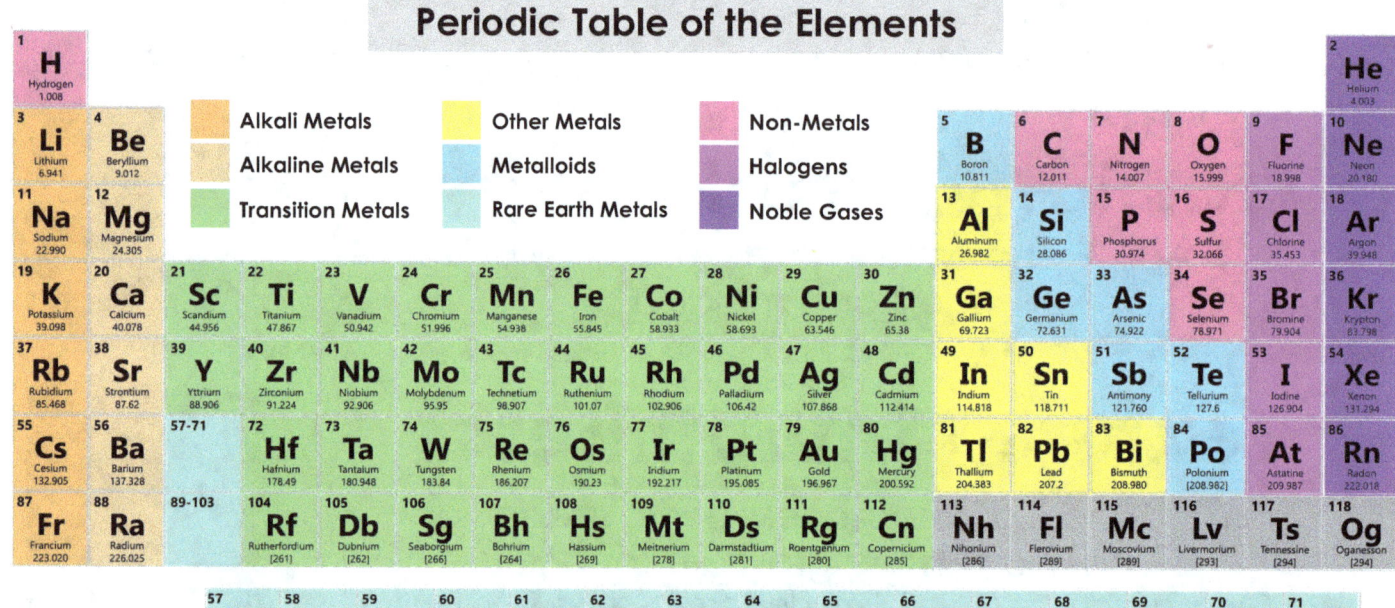

Important Elements for Potters

Primary Function	Type of Element	Comments
Flux (Melting Agents)	Alkali Metals	Alkali metals, such as sodium, potassium and lithium, can act as a flux.
Flux (Melting Agents)	Alkaline Metals	Alkaline earth metals, such as magnesium and calcium, are used as fluxes. Magnesium carbonate is a flux and colorant.
Colorants	Transition Metals	Transition metals, such as chromium, manganese, iron, cobalt and nickel are colorants for clay and glaze. Zinc oxide is a flux and opacifier.
Colorants	Rare Earth Metals	Rare earth metals, such as neodymium, erbium and praseodymium, are used as colorants in glass and glazes. Glazes can have vivid colors and maintain transparency.
Stabilizing Agent	Other Metals	Alumina is a stiffening/stabilizer. Lead and bismuth can be used as fluxes. Tin is an opacifier.
Glass Formers	Metalloids	Silica and boron are glass formers. Clay and glaze need a glass former that reacts when heated. Boron also acts as a flux.
Water	Non-Metals	Hydrogen and oxygen form water and are found in all clay and glazes. Selenium and arsenic are colorants. Phosphorus a flux. Carbon is a key component in several colorants such as cobalt carbonate.

www.artboxadventures.net   artboxadventures@gmail.com

Chapter 1: Attributes of Clay

Stages of Clay

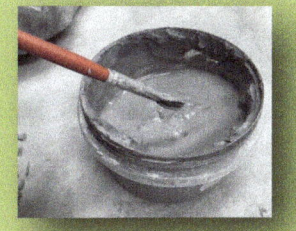

Slip/Slurry
Clay mixed with water into a pudding-like or liquid consistency.
Used for joining clay, slip trailing, and slip casting.

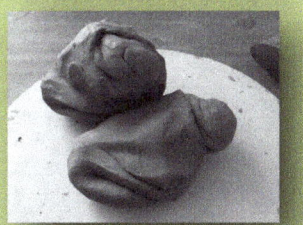

Plastic
Soft, workable clay that can be easily molded and formed.
Used for hand-building, extruding and wheel throwing.

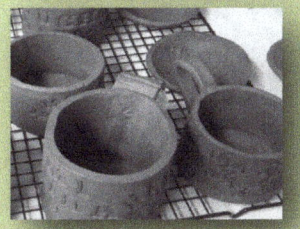

Leather-Hard
Clay that has hardened slightly.
This is the ideal stage for carving clay and building tall slab constructions.

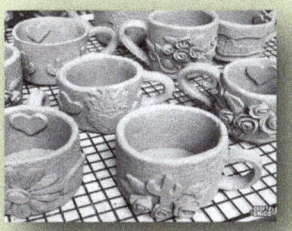

Bone-Dry
Clay that is completely dried and ready to be fired.
Clay is very fragile at this stage.

Recyclable

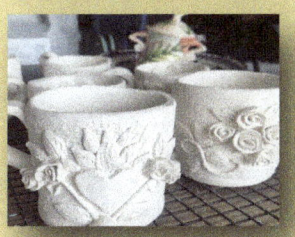

Bisqueware
Clay that has been transformed into ceramic material after being fired once.
Ready to be glazed, stained or painted.

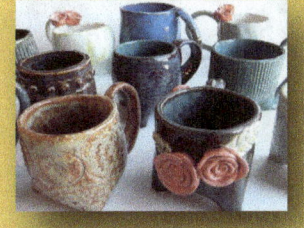

Glazeware
Ceramic material with glaze applied and fired a second time.

Non-Recyclable

www.artboxadventures.net · artboxadventures@gmail.com

Chapter 1: Attributes of Clay

The Ceramic Process

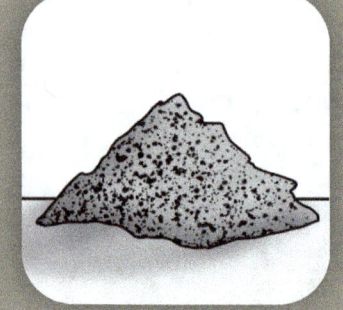
Preparing Raw Materials
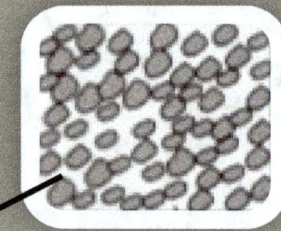
Clay Powders
Air

Add Water

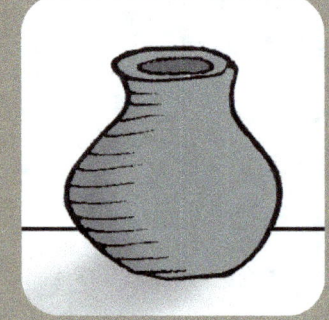
Making & Shaping the Wet Clay
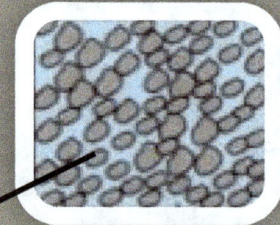
Wet Clay
Water

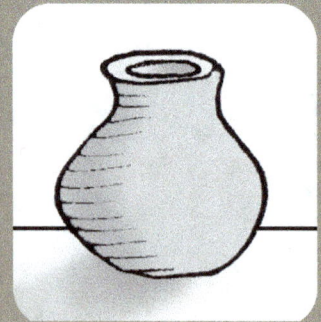
Drying the Clay
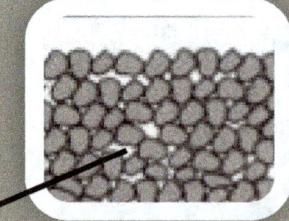
Dried Clay
Air Pores

Add Heat by Firing in a Kiln

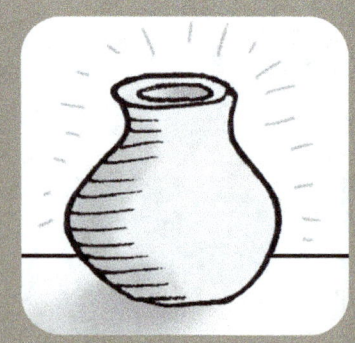
Firing the Clay
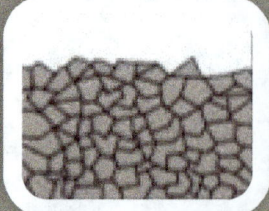
Fired Clay

Chapter 1: Attributes of Clay

What is Glaze?

Glaze is...

the glassy surface that make ceramics functional and colorful.

Geologically

Geologically, the raw materials used to make glaze are mined in many of the same places as clay. These raw materials are processed and combined in the certain ratios to make glazes.

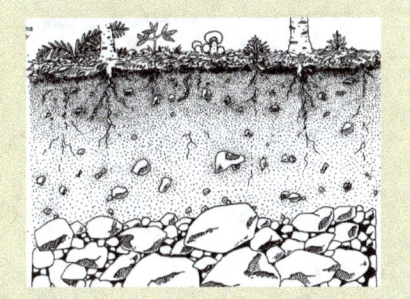

Chemically

Chemically, glaze is a combination of silica, alumina, and flux along with some other minerals/substances that give glaze color and opacity.

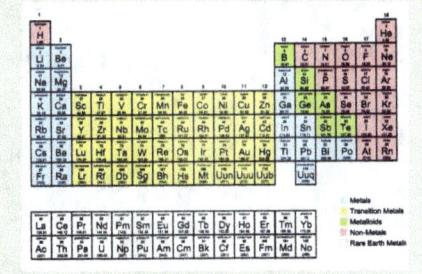

Physically

Physically, glaze is dramatically changed by heat. Silica is the glass former, the alumina is the stiffener that keeps the molten glass from flowing off the artwork and the flux is the melting agent. Glazes often have other additives including colorants, opacifies and suspending agents that impact the way they look.

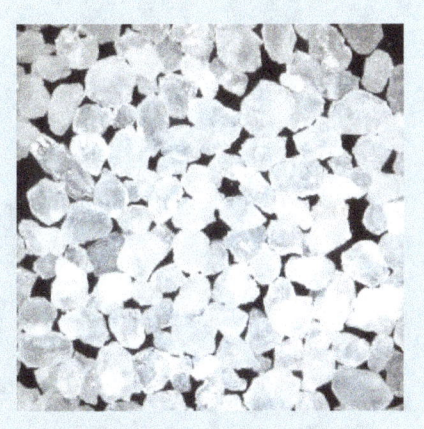

Artistically

Artistically, glaze is a crushed glass-like liquid that once heated, adds color and degree of shine to clay artworks. Glaze adheres to porous ceramic surfaces, and can make them waterproof and food safe.

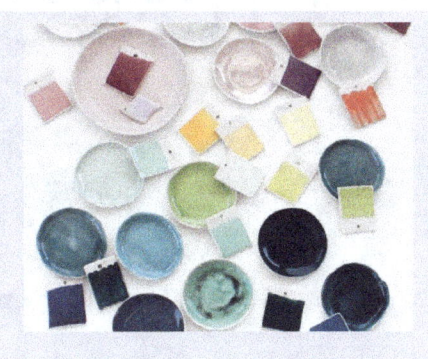

www.artboxadventures.net   artboxadventures@gmail.com

Chapter 1: Attributes of Clay

Properties of Glaze

Potters need to consider several important properties of glazes when selecting which glaze(s) they will use to finish their artwork. These include color, opacity, surface finish and firing temperature. Some glazes can be used and applied to achieve a variety of different special effects.

Color

Glazes can be formulated to produce a wide variety of colors using stains or metallic coloring oxides. Color is a major defining characteristic in describing any glaze.

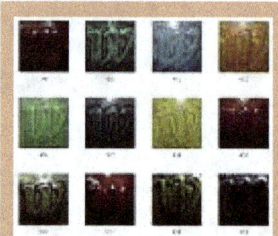

Opacity
(Light Transmission)

The ability of light to penetrate the glaze layer determines if a glaze is transparent, semi-opaque or opaque. With transparent glazes, what is underneath can show through.

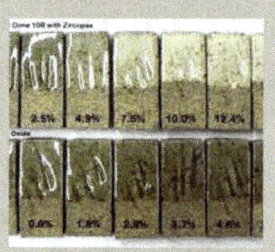

Surface Finish
(Texture)

Glazes can have various degrees of shine.
Gloss - high shine, smooth
Satin - low shine, semi-smooth
Matte - no shine, slightly rough

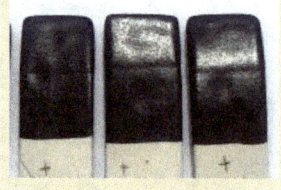

Firing Temperature
(Cone)

The 3 most common temperature ranges in ceramics are Cone 06 (1830°F), Cone 6 (2232°F) and Cone 9 (2336°F).

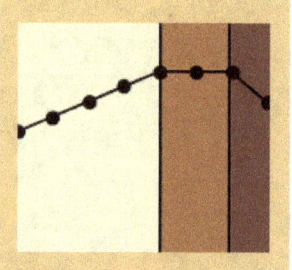

Special Effects

Glazes can be developed for wood, soda, salt, luster, raku, crystalline and other firing techniques.

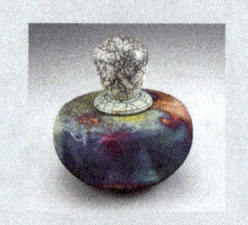

Chapter 1: Attributes of Clay

Glaze Chemistry

What are the Main Components of Glaze?

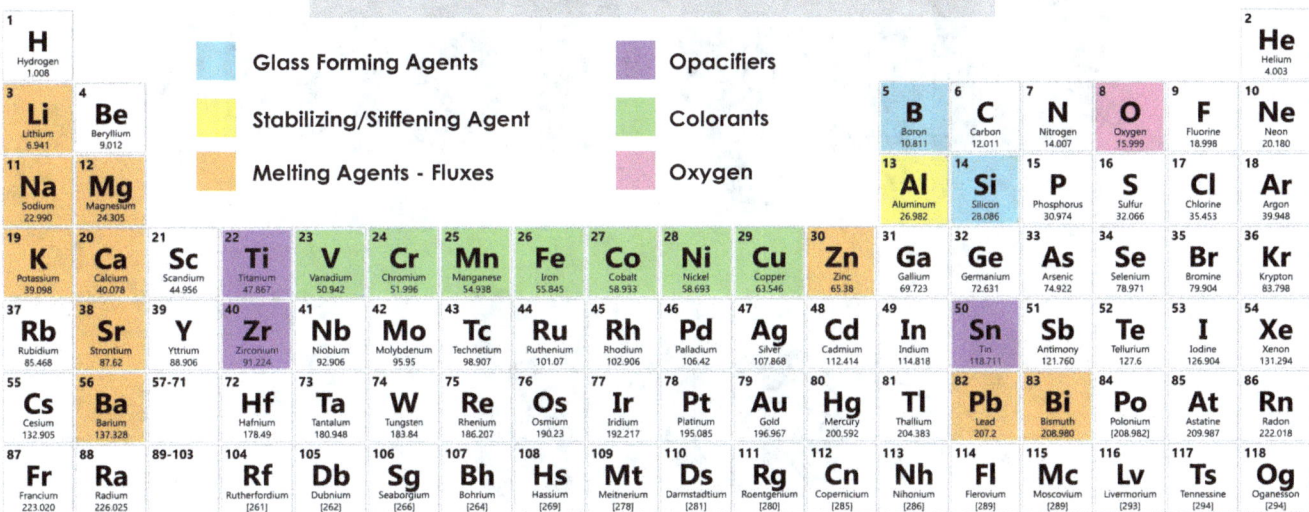

Periodic Table of the Elements

- Glass Forming Agents
- Stabilizing/Stiffening Agent
- Melting Agents - Fluxes
- Opacifiers
- Colorants
- Oxygen

Essential Glaze Components

Glass-Forming Agents	Stabilizing Agent (Refractory)	Melting Agents (Flux)
Silica silicon dioxide or boron trioxide	**Alumina** aluminum oxide	Various options include calcium oxide, potassium oxide, sodium oxide
Silica needs to be heated to a very high temperature (about 3100 F or 1710 C) to turn to glass. This is hotter than can be reached by ceramic kilns.	Alumina stiffens a glaze so it won't slide off and helps disperse fine gas bubbles that can form in the firing process.	Flux is need to lower the melting point of the higher temperature ingredients in a glaze.

Glaze Additives

Colorants	Opacifiers	Other
Made mostly from metallic oxides such as iron, manganese, cobalt, nickel, and	Common opacifiers include tin oxide, zirconium, titanium, zinc and bone ash.	Suspending agents, gums, and glaze thinners are also sometimes added.

Oxygen

Oxygen is present in all glazes. Various elements combine with oxygen to form oxides such as

Tin Oxide SnO_2

Calcium Oxide CaO

Silicon Oxide SiO_2

Aluminum Oxide Al_2O_3

Note: Some oxides impact a glaze in more than one way. For example, iron oxide acts as flux agent and a colorant.

Chapter 2: Clay Tools and Equipment

Clay Tools and Equipment

Clay Tools & Equipment Types, Parts and How to Use Them

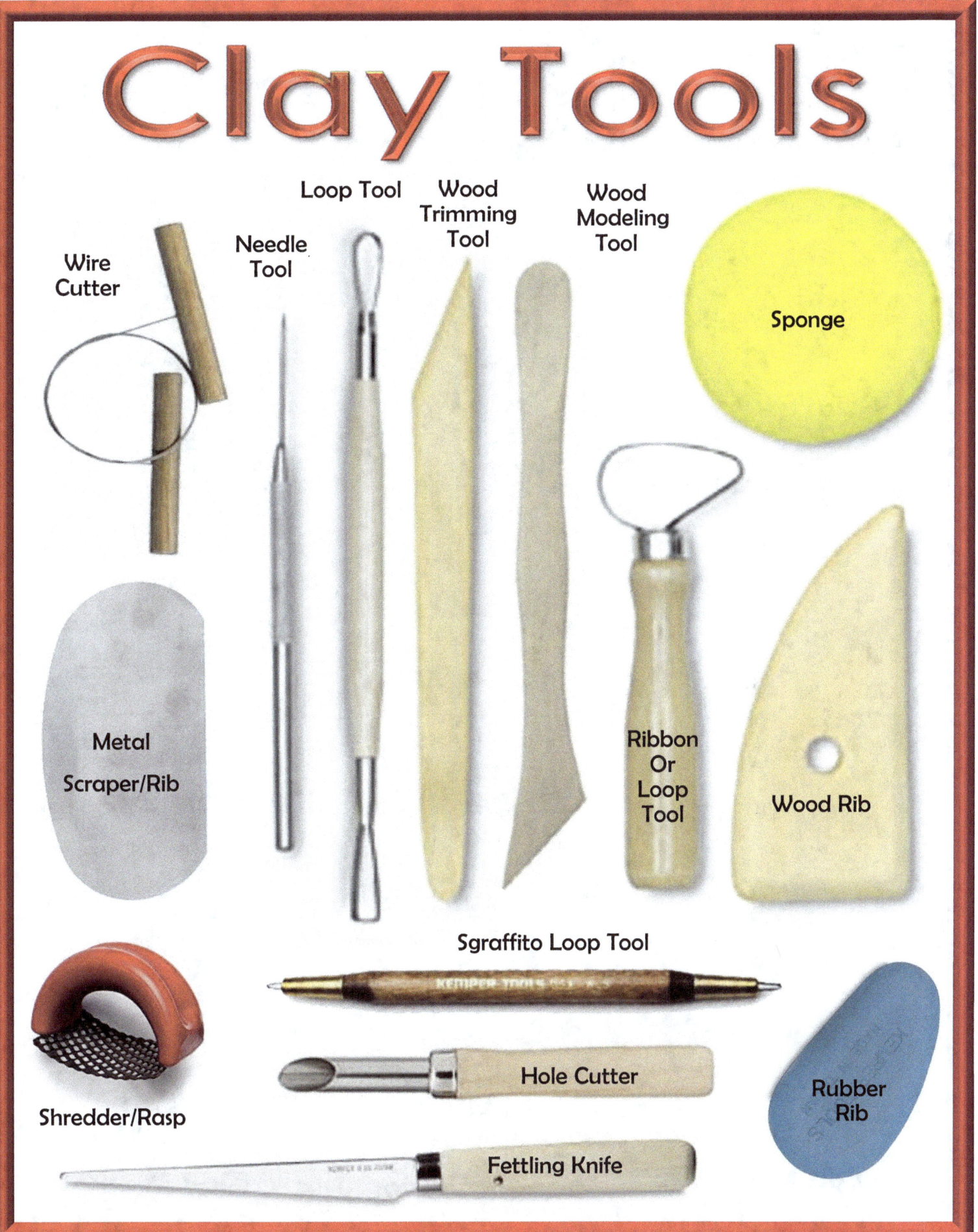

Clay Equipment

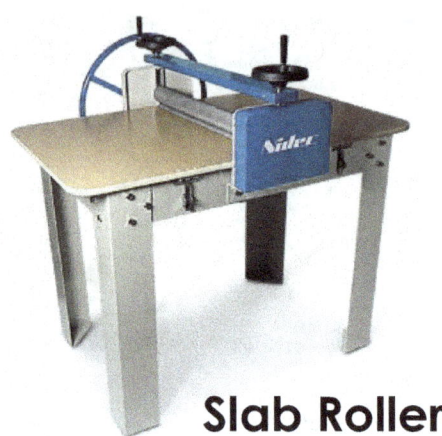
Slab Roller

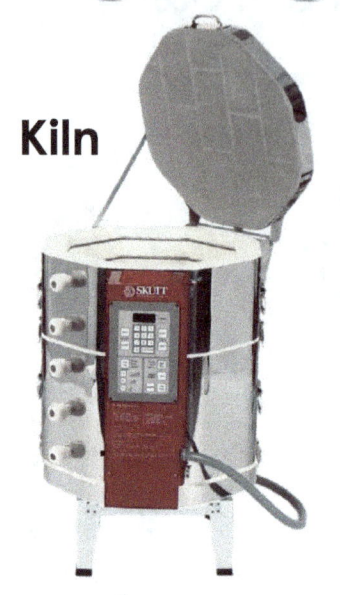
Kiln

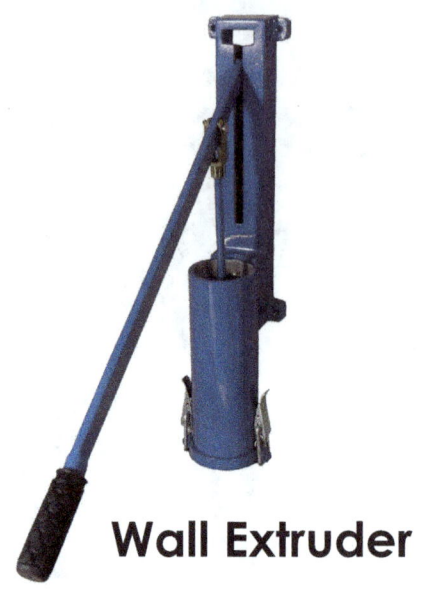
Wall Extruder

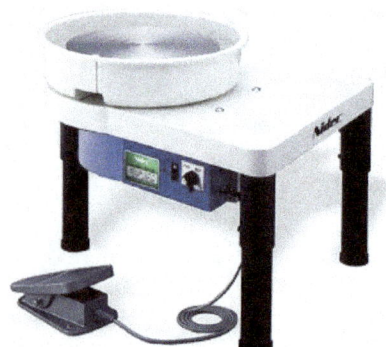
Pottery Wheel

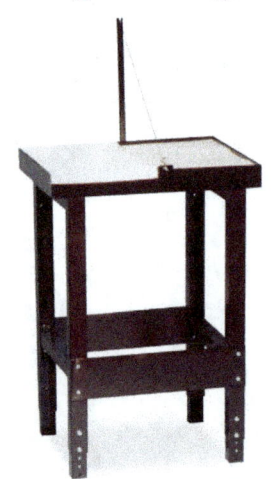
Wedging Table

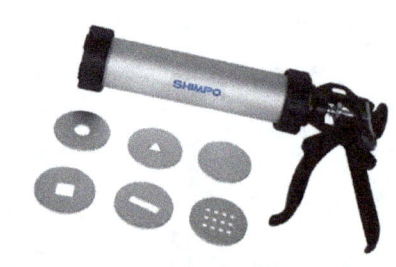
Handheld Extruder

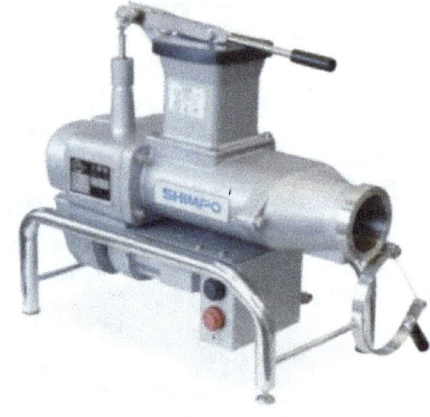
Pug Mill

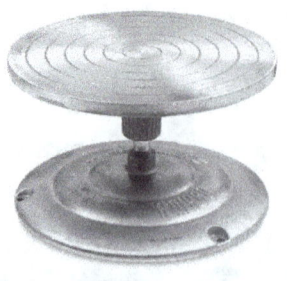
Banding Wheel

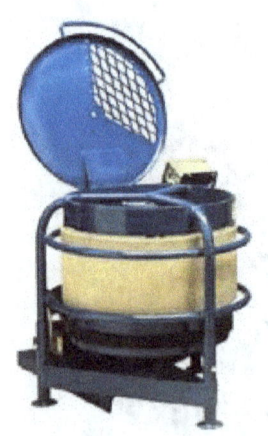
Clay Mixer

Tools to Create Slabs

SLAB: 'A Flat Even Piece of Clay'

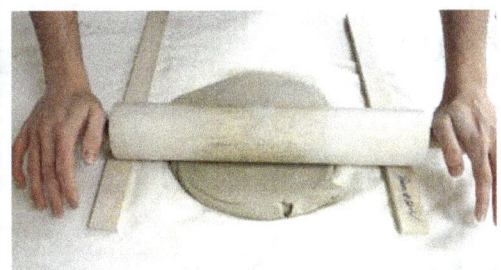

Rolling Pins

Rolling pins are an inexpensive tool often made of wood. They are generally used with slats to ensure uniform thickness of the slab and to make sure the slab is not too thin.

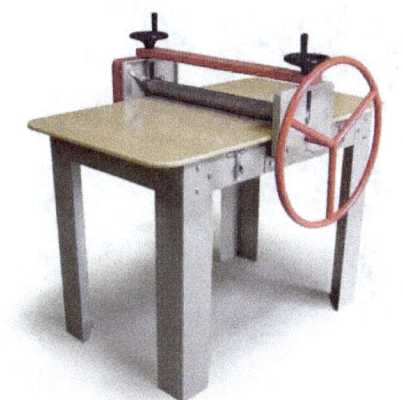

Stand-Alone Slab Rollers

Stand-alone slab rollers are supported by legs. They are large and durable, making them ideal for schools and bigger, busy studios.

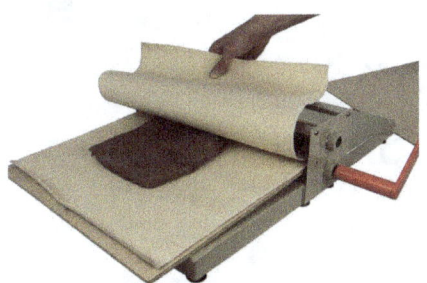

Tabletop Slab Rollers

Portable, smaller slab rollers are great for smaller classrooms and studios and are less expensive.

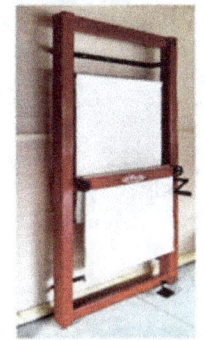

Vertical Slab Rollers

Unique slab rollers that can be mounted on a wall or on a narrow cart. This type can save space in a studio/classroom.

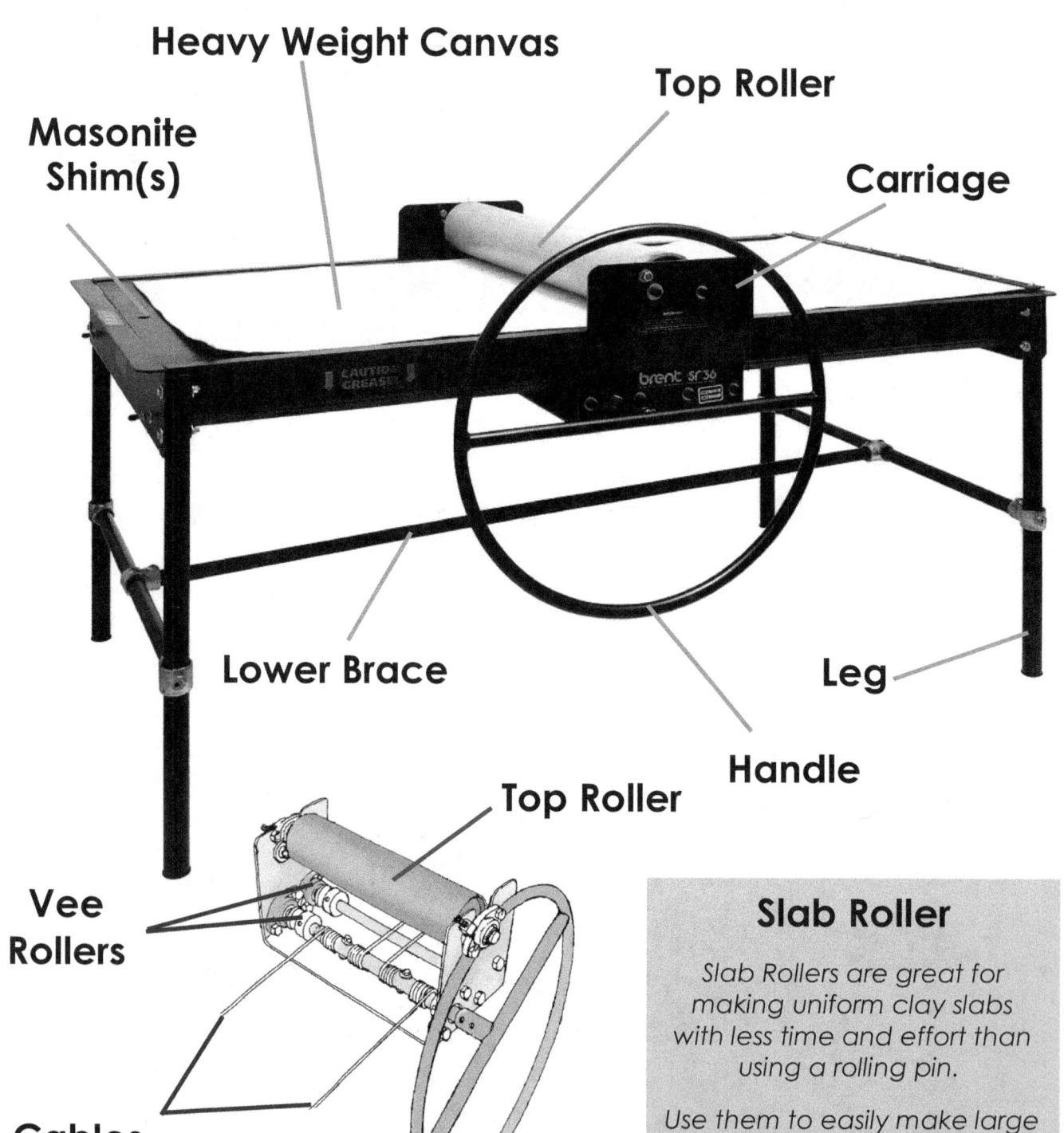

Chapter 2: Clay Tools and Equipment

Tips for Using a Slab Roller

1. **Wedge Clay** to remove air bubbles and improve the consistency of clay. For best results use plastic (soft, wet) clay, but not too moist.

2. **Shape the Clay** into a 'loaf' (fat hot dog) with your hands. The loaf should be a bit wider than the width needed for your artwork.

3. **Set the thickness on the slab roller** (if not already set). You may need to start thicker and work towards a 1/2" with each pass.

4. **Place the clay loaf between two pieces of canvas.** Covering the clay with canvas prevents the clay from sticking to the roller or table.

5. **Taper the edge of the clay.** To make it easier for the clay to fit under the clay roller, pat one edge of the clay with your hand so that it tapers. Position the clay next to the roller so the tapered edge is closest to the roller.

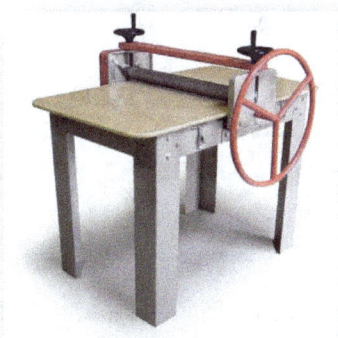

6. **Turn Handle.** As you bein turning the handle, the clay and canvas should start moving through the rollers. If it isn't moving, check the settings on the roller and the thickness of the clay.

7. **Flatten Clay.** Once the clay and canvas has start moving through the rollers, continue cranking until the clay has completely passed through the roller. Some slab rollers require rolling the handle back the other direction to removed the clay.

8. **Multiple Pass-Throughs.** Do additional pass-throughs with the clay, rotating the clay each time.
    - This makes the slab wider/rounder and creates multiple direction grain structure. With each pass-through, it is recommended to lift the clay and reposition it.
    - On some slab rollers, you will need to use the adjustment knobs and pointers to narrow the gap between the rollers.
    - With other slab rollers, you can add a board or shim to decrease the space between the rollers.
    - Note: Unidirectional grain structure can cause drying and shrinkage issues.

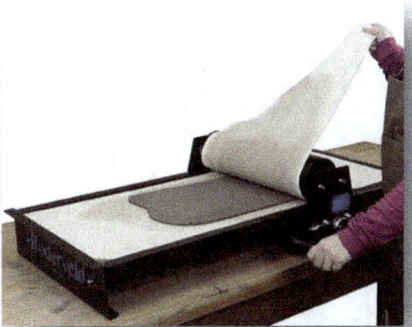

www.artboxadventures.net   artboxadventures@gmail.com

Chapter 2: Clay Tools and Equipment

Types of Clay Extruders

Extruders Come In 3 Main Sizes

Besides varying in size, extruder produce different types, sizes and shapes of extruded clay and vary in price.

1. <u>Large Mounted Extruder:</u>

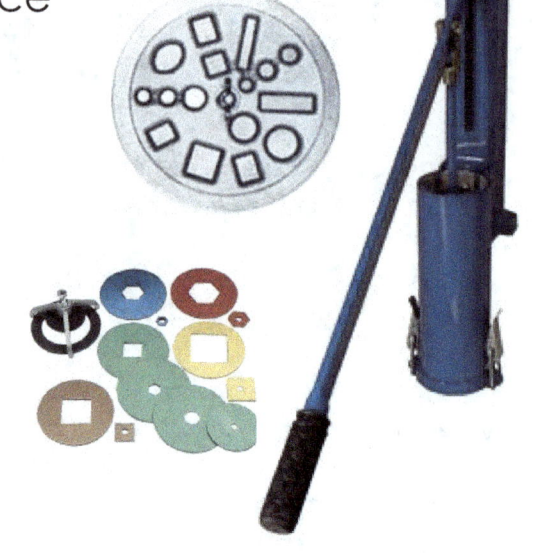

- Heavy duty tool
- Often mounted on wall or table
- Ideal for making large hollow forms
- Makes lots of 'coils' at one time
- Barrels can be square or round
- Barrels are usually 4-6" in diameter
- $$$

2. <u>Medium Clay Gun:</u>

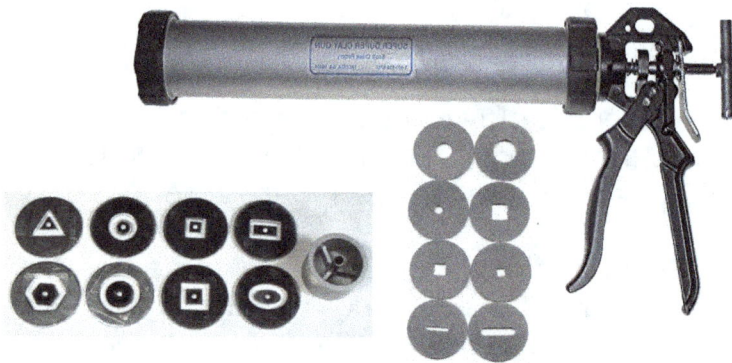

- Handheld and easy to use
- Ideal for making a variety of smaller coils
- Can make hollow forms with a die-holder kit
- Barrel is about 2" in diameter
- $$

3. <u>Small Mini Extruder:</u>

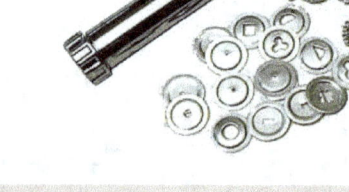

- Good for creating details and texture
- Great for making hair and fur
- Barrel is about 1/2" in diameter
- $

Tips for Using an Extruder

- Always use moist, well-wedged clay.
- Clean extruder, die and die-holder thoroughly.
- Do not store clay in an extruder.

Note: Hardened, dry clay makes cleaning and future use difficult.

Chapter 2: Clay Tools and Equipment

Anatomy of a Handheld Extruder

Handheld extruders can create both solid and hollow clay forms

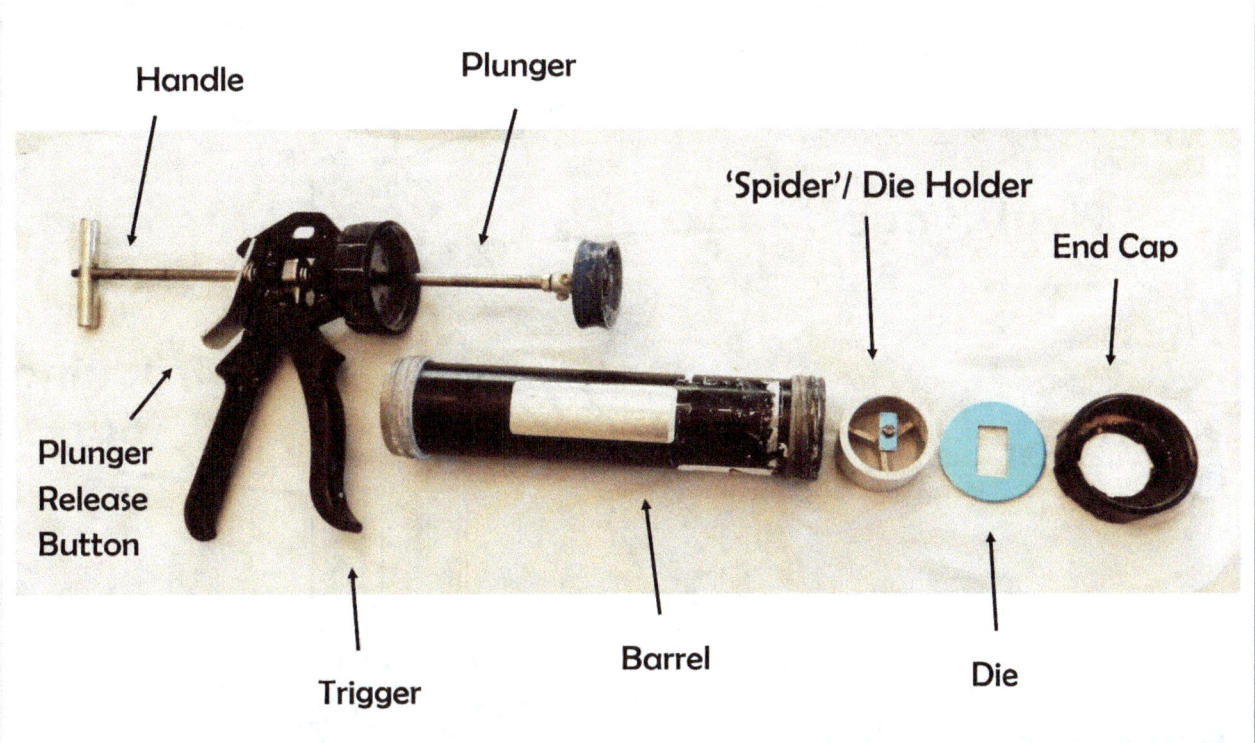

Labels: Handle, Plunger, 'Spider'/ Die Holder, End Cap, Plunger Release Button, Trigger, Barrel, Die

Clay Extruders

Extruders have interchangeable dies with holes that come in a variety of sizes and shapes.

Each die shape produces different results.

Hollow forms can be created with an inner die-holder ('spider').

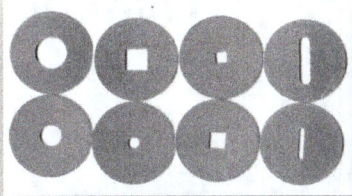

Various Dies & Die-Holder

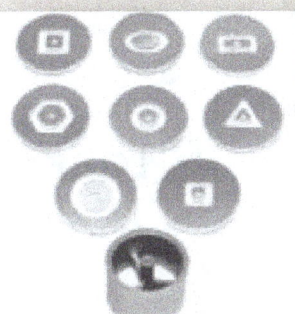

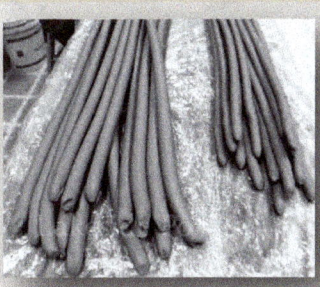

Produce Solid & Hollow Forms

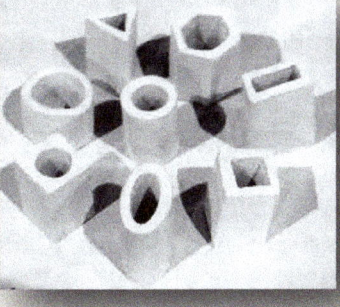

www.artboxadventures.net | 25 | artboxadventures@gmail.com

Chapter 2: Clay Tools and Equipment

Anatomy of a Wall Extruder

Extrude: "The act or process of shaping by forcing through a die."

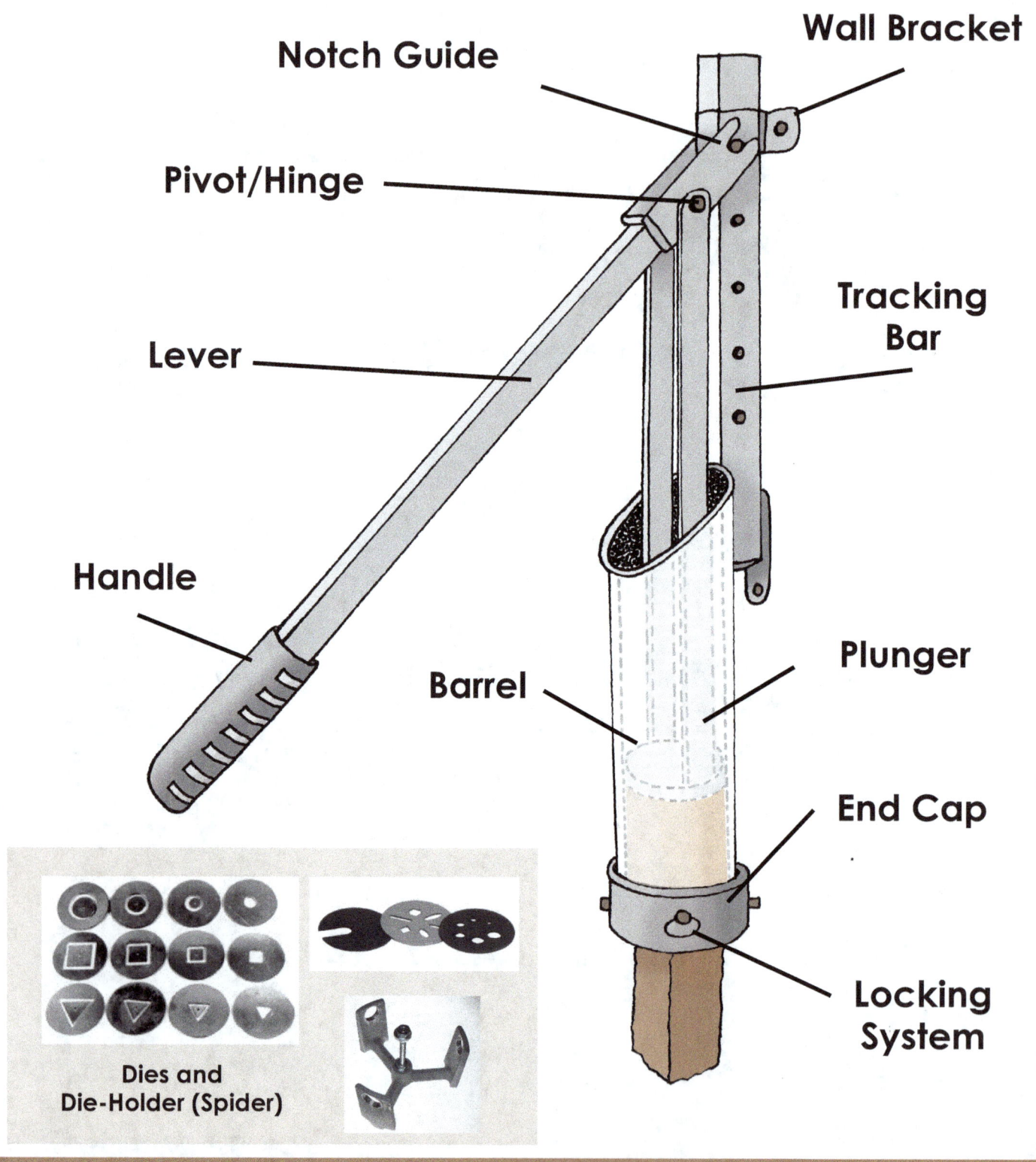

- Wall Bracket
- Notch Guide
- Pivot/Hinge
- Lever
- Tracking Bar
- Handle
- Barrel
- Plunger
- End Cap
- Locking System

Dies and Die-Holder (Spider)

Tips for Using an Extruder

Key Steps

1. Use moist, well-wedged clay. Soft clay is very important when extruding.
2. Mold clay into a cylinder shape a little narrower than the barrel of the extruder.
3. Remove the extruder cap and put in the die. Use die holder (spider) if making a hollow form. Secure the cap with the locking system.
4. Put wedged clay into the top of the barrel.
5. Guide the plunger into the top of the barrel so it is resting on the loaded clay.

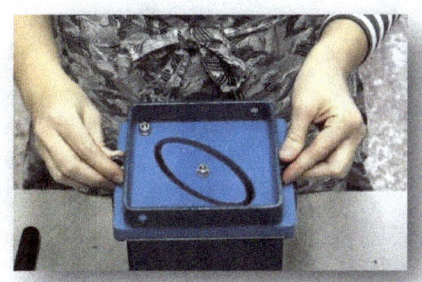

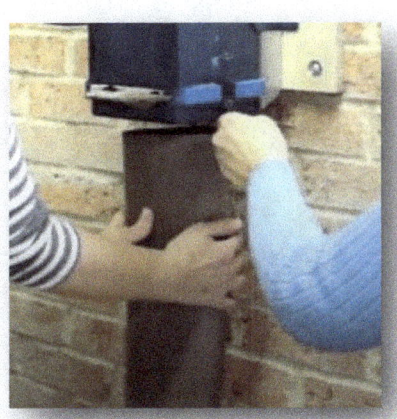

6. Make sure the notch guide is positioned in the tracking bar to ensure the plunger moves only up and down and creates the axis where the lever raises and lowers.
7. Pull down on the lever with firm, slow pressure. You may need to lower the notch guide and pull the lever down several times before clay begins to come out.
8. As the clay comes out, it often starts to curve to one side. You might want to cut off the first part. Cut it off squarely. Lower the notch guide, pulling the lever all the way down until no clay comes out.
9. Empty the barrel of the extruder and remove the extruder cap with die (and die holder/spider if used).
10. Clean the extruder, cap and any dies. An extruder and dies will last longer if they are well cared for.

Other Extruder Tips

1. **Die Placement.** If you want straight extrusions, make sure the extruder die is centered in the barrel. When making a hollow form, the internal die pieces have to be centered so the walls are of even thickness. If you want curved extrusions, try putting the die off to one side.
2. **Use a paddle or tube to help square up artwork.** Square extrusions can be straightened by using small flat boards as support on the inside and/or outside while you paddle the sides. For a cylindrical extrusion, try using a paper covered tube that fits inside.
3. **Remove clay before it dries.** Do not let clay dry on the plunger, die, die holder (spider) or in the barrel. Dry clay is doubly hard to remove.
4. **Small-Opening Dies.** Apply more leverage for small-opening dies. If you are struggling you may need moister clay. Consider making a "gang" die to make coils more easily. Extruding a single, small-diameter coil can be very difficult if your extruder has a large barrel; using a four-place coil die (gang) can make it easier.

Chapter 2: Clay Tools and Equipment

Anatomy of a Potter's Wheel

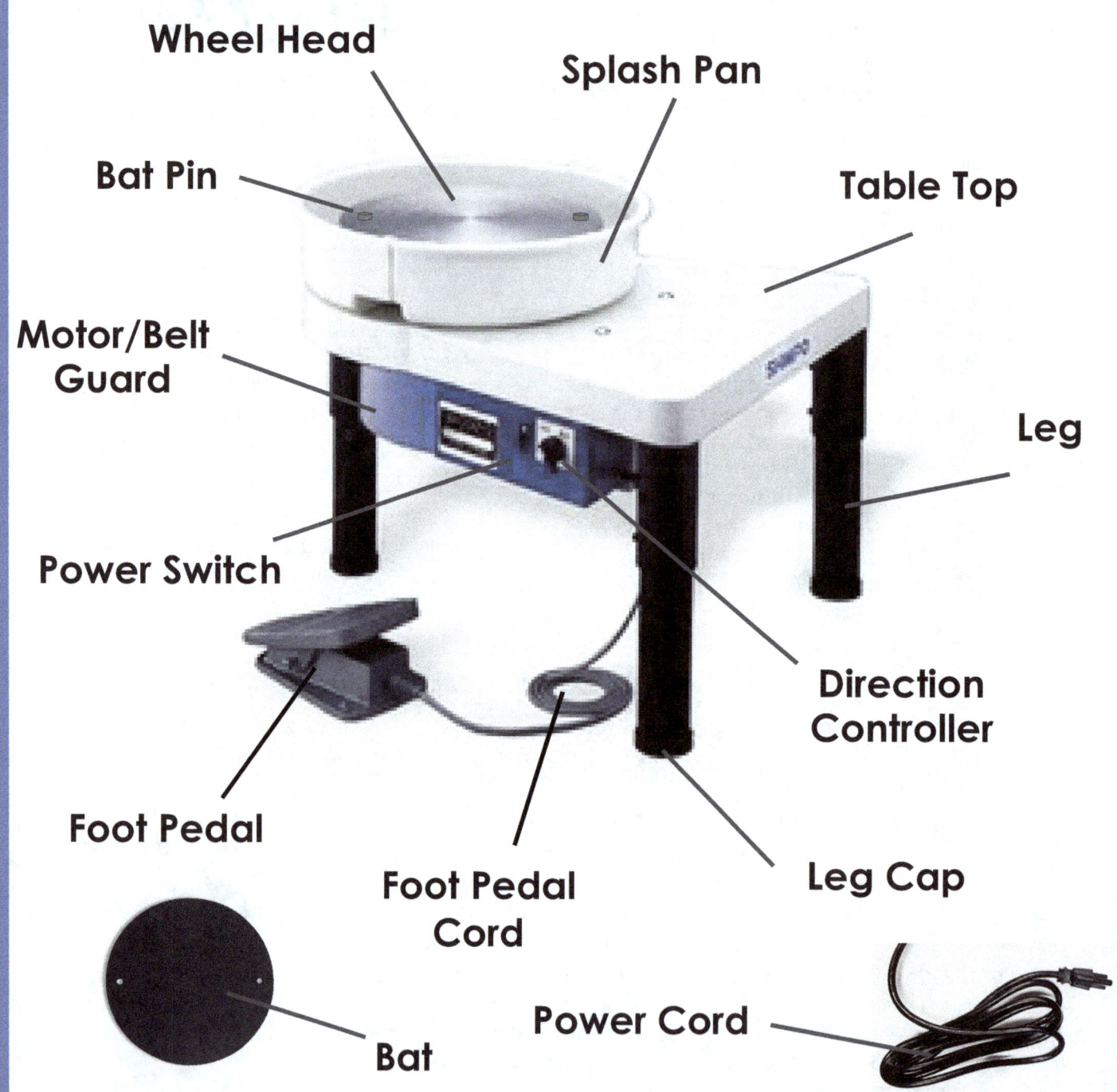

Chapter 2: Clay Tools and Equipment

Wheel Pottery Tools

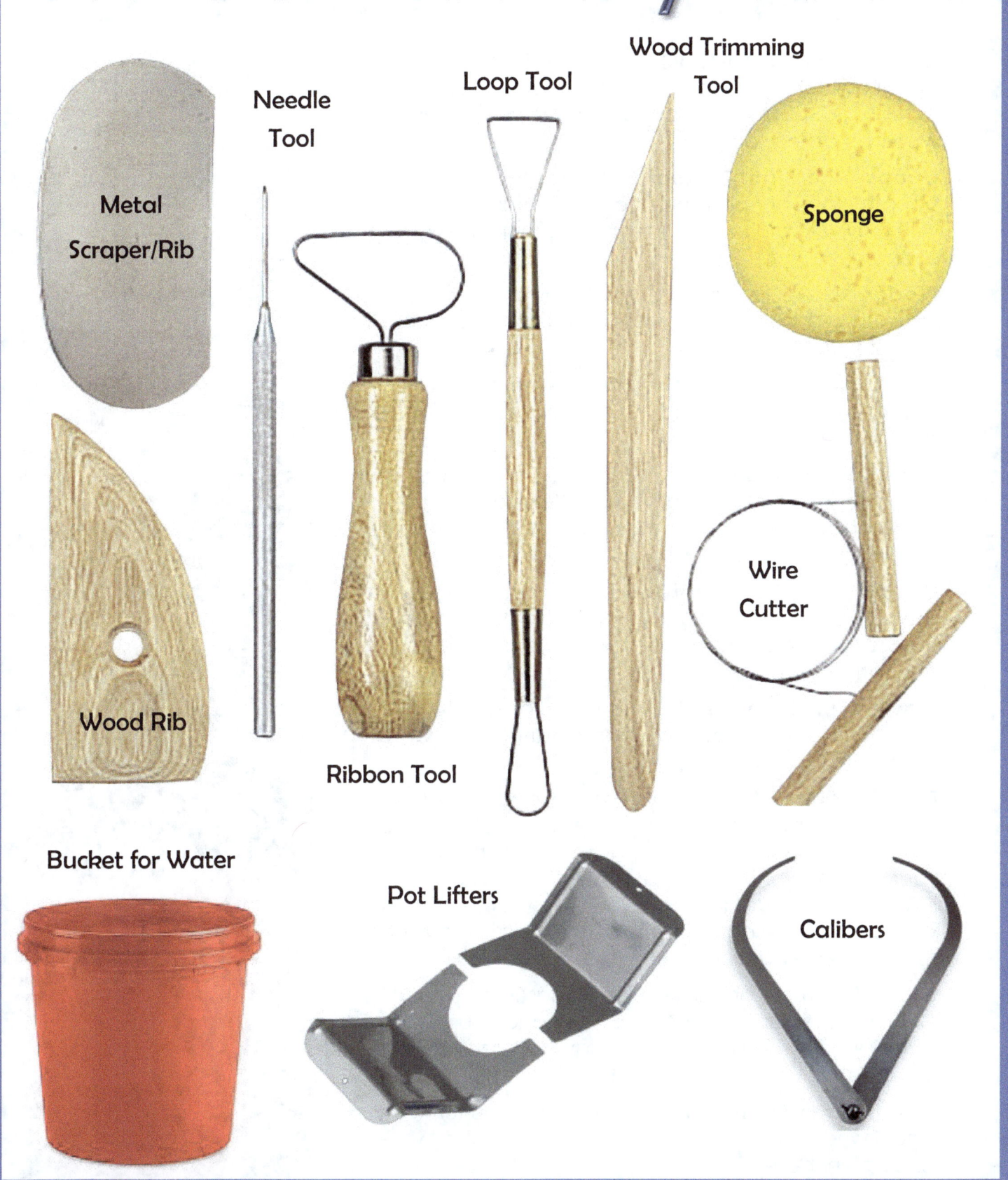

Chapter 2: Clay Tools and Equipment

Tips for Using the Potter's Wheel

- **Get Out the Tools You Will Need:** You will need a bucket about half full of water, as well as some pottery tools including a sponge, wire cutter, needle tool, rib and wood modeling tool.

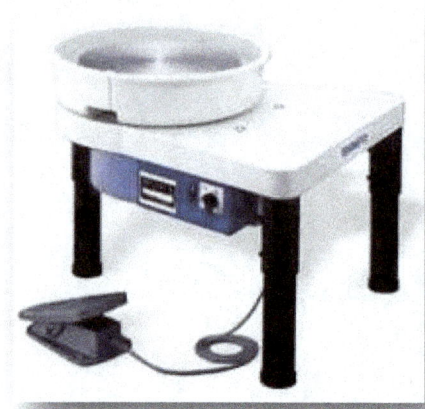

- **Choose the Right Type of Clay:** Most potters use smooth clays, but beginners can find it easier to work with clay with a bit of grog or sand as it is less likely to collapse.

- **Wedge Clay:** Wedging your clay well is important as it removes air pockets and small hard spots, and gives clay uniform consistency.

- **Clay Should Be Well Attached to the Wheel or Bat:** It works best if the clay you put on the wheel is rounded and not flat on the bottom.

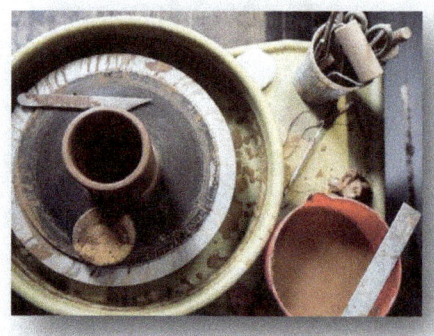

- **Use Plenty of Water:** If your clay feels dry against your hands as you're centering, you don't have enough water on your hands. Your clay can become too wet if you use too much water.

- **Pay Attention to Wheel Speed:** You want to speed the wheel up to med-high or high for centering and then reduce to a slower speed when your are forming the pottery.

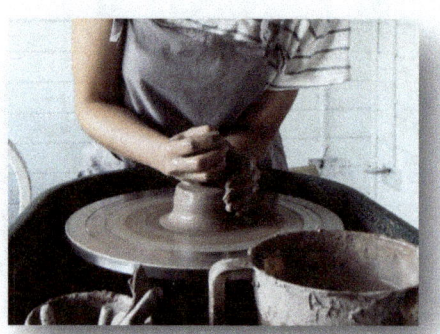

- **Move Your Hands SLOWLY:** It is important to move your hands slowly as clay can easily go off center with quick movements.

- **Pay Attention to Your Body Position:** A good body position is important. Place your legs as close to your splash pan as possible. Keep your arms anchored and your back straight. Lean your body into the clay. Keeping your arms anchored to your leg or the side of your body helps a lot — that way the clay has nowhere to go except where you want it.

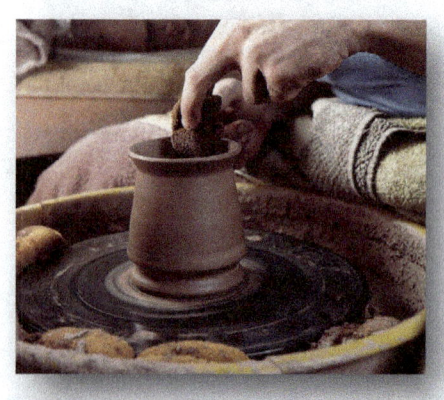

- **Clean Up:** There are quite a few things to clean including the wheel head, tools, shelf and yourself. Don't put clay down the drain. Clay and slip/slurry can be recycled.

- **Turn On and Off the Wheel:** Of course you turn on the wheel when using it, but don't forget to turn it off when you are finished.

Chapter 2: Clay Tools and Equipment

Anatomy of a Pug Mill

A pug mill is a special electric powered machine used to recycle and reclaim clay. It can process a lot of clay in a short period of time.

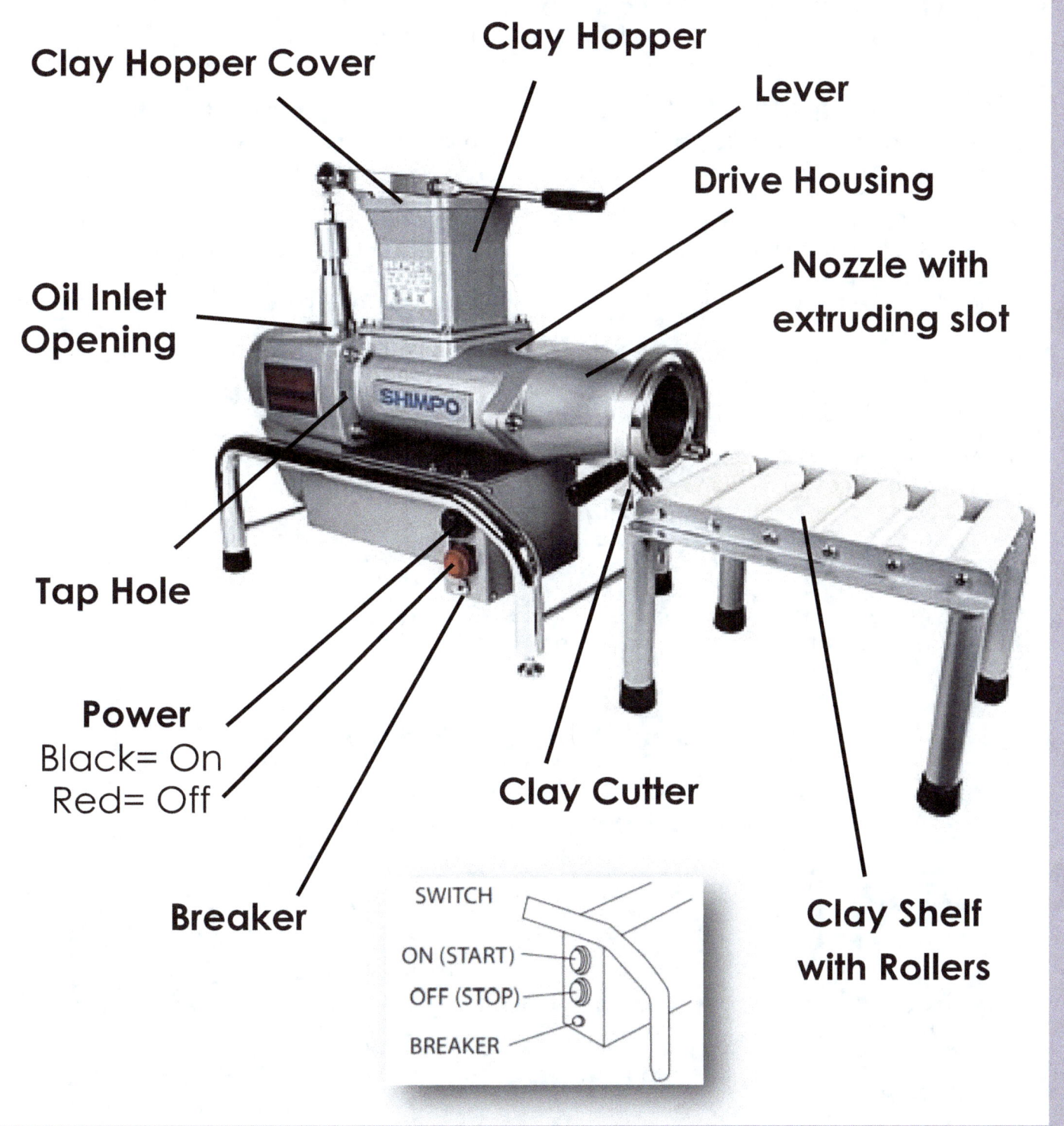

Chapter 2: Clay Tools and Equipment

Pug Mill Tips

CAUTION - WARNING
Pugmills are incredibly powerful machines. Used properly, a pugmill is a very safe and effective machine, but no one should operate a pugmill without being trained and fully aware of the risks.

Steps for Pugging Clay
(Some machines also mix clay)
1. Remove the extrusion nozzle cover and open the hopper.
2. Place clay into the clay hopper in small amounts. On de-airing machines, make sure the hopper lid can close.
3. If clay is a bit dry, add some water gradually.
4. Lower the hopper cover (wipe lid and hopper rim if you are using a pugmill with vacuum chamber).
5. Turn the power on.
6. Add more clay and water as needed.
7. Use the clay cutter to cut the pugged clay as it comes out. Cut off the extrusions when they are about 18" long. By keeping a small table in the clay mixing room, you can either stack the pugs on that table or put them straight into your clay barrel.
8. Switch the power off when you are finished processing clay.

Clean Up (Immediately after mixing/pugging Clay)
1. Clean clay residue from the outside of the pugmill.
2. Put nozzle cover on (if you don't have a cover, place sponge over nozzle and secure plastic over opening).
3. Lower cover over the hopper opening (to keep the clay moist, you might place a damp sponge in first).

Deep Cleaning and Disassembly Procedures
When total cleaning of the pug mill is desired, remove all clay from the internal parts of the main body by following the disassembly procedures provided by the manufacturer.

Clay Mixer vs. Pug Mill

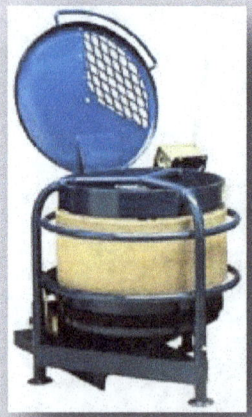

A clay mixer works the clay and mixes it thoroughly distributing water throughout the clay until it's at a workable consistency. A pug mill recycles clay. If you need clay that's ready to throw without any further wedging, you'll need a de-airing pug mill either as a standalone machine or as part of a mixer/pug mill. Some pug mills are also mixers.

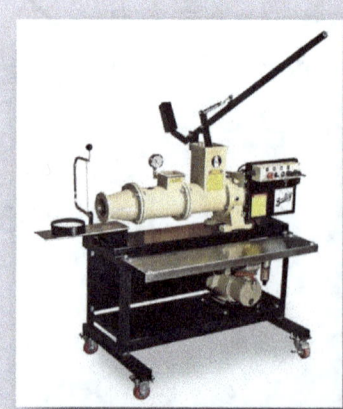

www.artboxadventures.net — artboxadventures@gmail.com

Chapter 2: Clay Tools and Equipment

Anatomy of a Kiln
with Kiln Furniture

Kiln Furniture

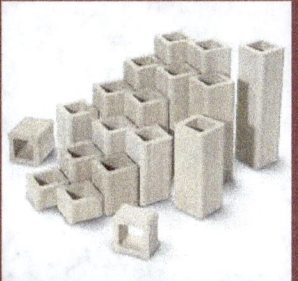
Kiln Shelves

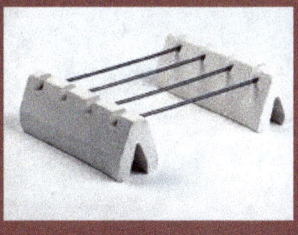
Kiln Posts

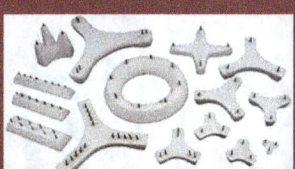
Bead Rack

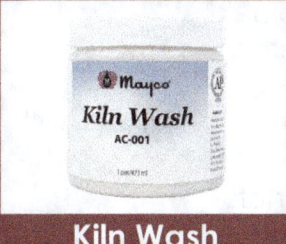
Stilts

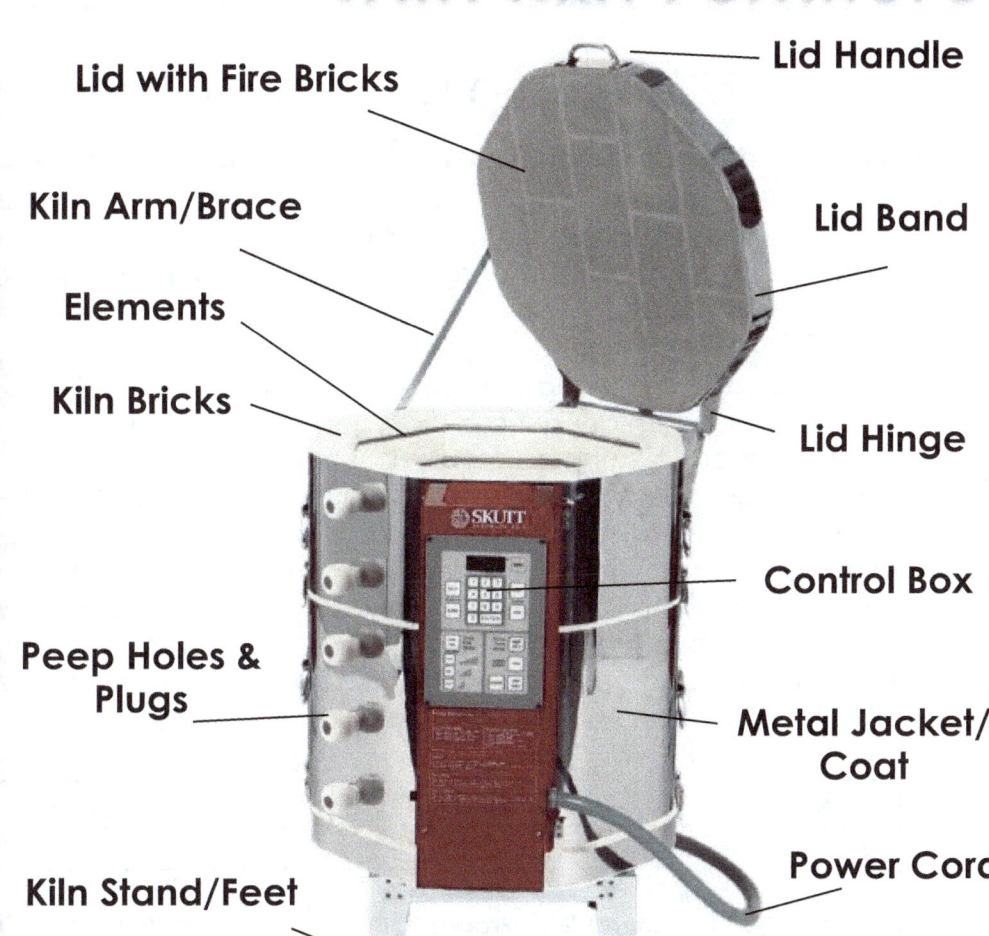
Kiln Wash

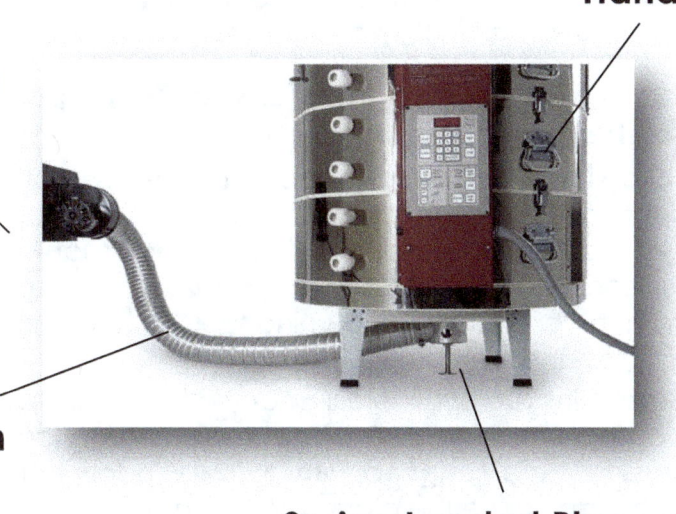

- Lid with Fire Bricks
- Lid Handle
- Kiln Arm/Brace
- Lid Band
- Elements
- Kiln Bricks
- Lid Hinge
- Control Box
- Peep Holes & Plugs
- Metal Jacket/Coat
- Kiln Stand/Feet
- Power Cord
- Wall Mounted Fan
- Handles
- Flexible Aluminum Duct
- Spring Loaded Plenum Cup

www.artboxadventures.net   artboxadventures@gmail.com

Types of Kilns

There are many different types of kilns.

Kilns Vary in their Power Source

The three most common types of kilns are electric, gas and wood.

- **Electric Kilns** are the most common type used in ceramics and are comparatively inexpensive. These kilns always fire in *oxidation,* meaning there's oxygen present in a completely controlled environment, which yields consistent results with glazes. This is important for potters who want to replicate their work.
- **Gas Kilns** run on natural gas, propane or butane. They fire in *reduction,* which doesn't allow oxygen in during firing. Reduction firing results can be unpredictable, but typically yield rich, earthy colors. It's difficult to maintain consistency, so gas kilns are better for one-of-a-kind creations.
- **Wood Kilns** are fueled by wood and have been used for thousands of years to make pottery. They're very labor-intensive because they need constant re-fueling to keep the fire at consistently high temperatures and often take much longer to fire. Many potters feel that the unique results are worth the extra work.

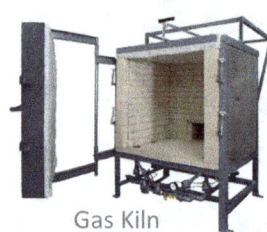
Electric Kiln

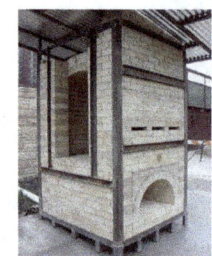
Gas Kiln

Kiln	Type	Examples
Power Source	Electric	Electric Kilns
	Gas Natural Gas, Propane, Butane	Gas Kilns Top Hat (Raku)
	Wood	Brick Kiln Pit Fire
	Other (Oil/Coal/Solar)	Homemade Kilns

Wood Kiln

Raku Kiln

Specialty kilns are designed for specific purposes. Raku and Glass are two of the most common.

- **Raku Kilns** yield a unique finish. Bisque-fired pottery is heated until is red hot and glaze is molten. Then each piece is placed in a bed of combustible materials and covered. The intense reduction and cooling result in crackle surfaces and metallic colors. Unglazed areas of the clay become black from the carbon in the burning fuel. Raku kilns are commonly powered by propane.
- **Glass Kilns** are available in many different shapes and sizes. Artists working with very large pieces may prefer a large oval design. Some glass kilns are designed with a view window or for easy access so artists can manipulate the glass while it is hot.

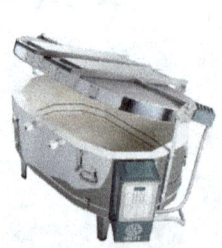
Glass Kiln

Chapter 2: Clay Tools and Equipment

Types of Kilns Continued

Kilns Vary in Size and Power Needs

Kiln	Type	Examples
Size	Table-Top	Jewelry Small Glass Kilns
	Free Standing	Electric and Gas Kilns
	Industrial	Large Production Kilns Car/Shuttle Kilns

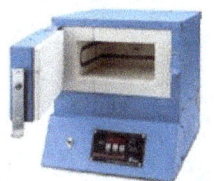
Table Top

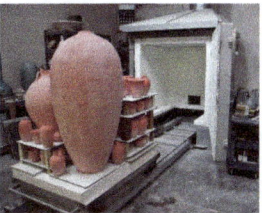
Industrial

Table-Top Kilns: These small kilns can sit on a table. They are ideal for jewelry making and enameling. They often have lower voltage (110 volts) and amperage (15-25 amps).

Free-Standing Kilns: These medium-sized kilns are the most common and use 220/240 voltage and 25-65 amps.

Walk-In Kilns: These kilns have plenty of room to fire many pieces and can accommodate extra big ceramic wares. They can be room size or even larger.

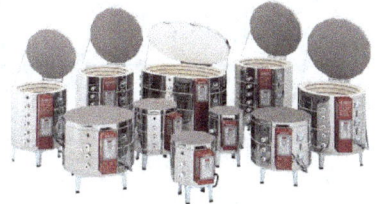
Free Standing

Kilns Vary in Loading Access

Kiln	Type	Examples
Loading Access	Front Loading	Many Gas Kilns
	Top Loading	Many Electric Kilns
	Full Access	Top Hat (Raku) Clamshell (Raku)

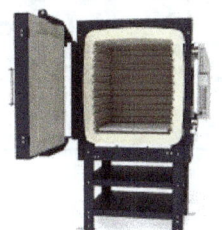
Front Loading

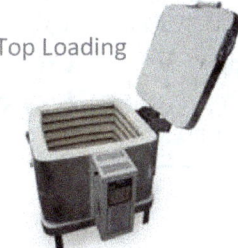
Top Loading

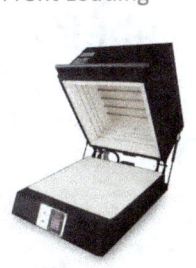
Clamshell

Top Hat

Front-Loading Kilns: Front-loading kilns are easier to load and generally more efficient for loading. They are more expensive, but are usually extremely durable and will have a longer life than top-loading kilns.

Top-Loading Kilns: Top-loading kilns are more difficult to load, especially tall versions if you are short. They are less expensive, which is one reason they are popular.

Full-Access Kilns: Full-access kilns include clamshell and top-hat kilns. Access from multiple angles is especially important when manipulating glass or removing hot raku pieces from the kiln.

Chapter 2: Clay Tools and Equipment

Types of Kilns Continued

Kilns Vary by their Shape

Types	Examples
Rounded	'Round'—Hexagonal Oval Kilns Bottle Kilns
Rectangular	Rectangular Kilns Square Kilns
Domed/Arched	Beehive (Anagama) Sprung Arch Kilns Catenary 'Cat' Kilns
Tunnel/Tubular	Car Kilns Climbing Kilns
Other	Pit Firing Brick/Barrell Kilns

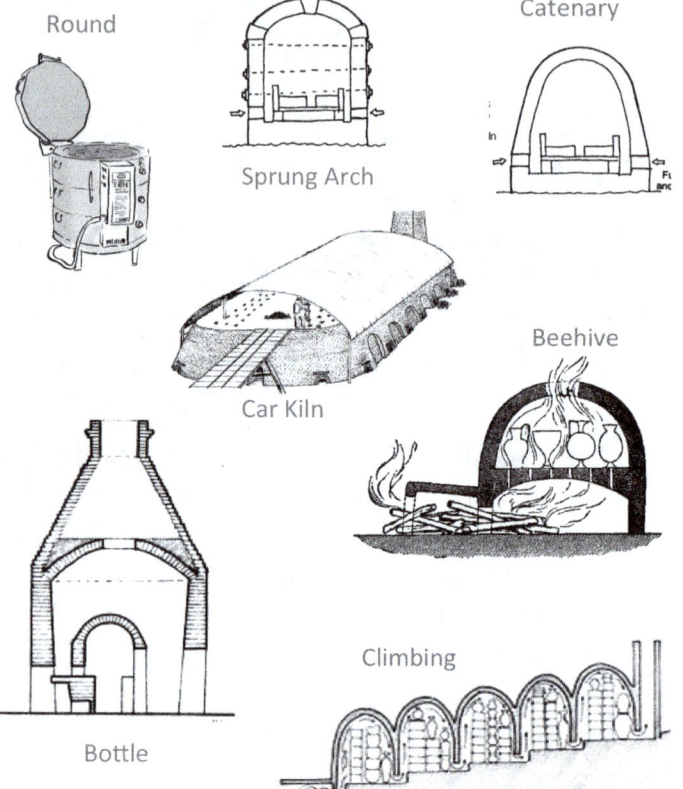

Round

Sprung Arch

Catenary

Car Kiln

Beehive

Bottle

Climbing

Kilns Vary in their Firing Cycle

Types	Examples
Continuous	Tunnel Kiln Commercial Kilns
Intermittent/Periodic (fired, cooled, reloaded)	Electric Kilns Gas Kilns

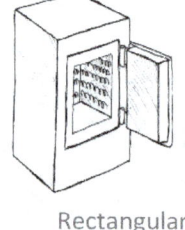

Rectangular

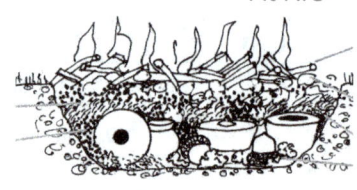

Pit Fire

Kilns Vary by their Heat Flow

Types	Examples
Up Draft	Gas Kilns
Down Draft	Gas Kilns
Cross Draft	Tunnel Kilns Climbing Kilns
Vented	Electric Kilns

Up Draft

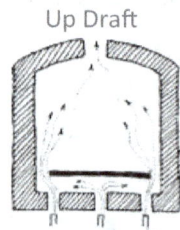

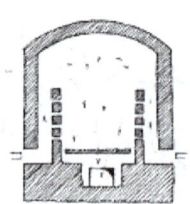

Down Draft

Cross Draft

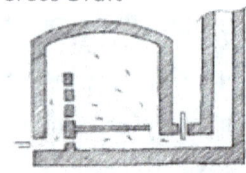

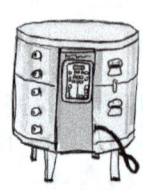

Vented

Kiln Loading Tips

1. Apply kiln wash to shelves as directed and only on one side.
2. Leave a 1" space between bottom shelf and the kiln floor.
3. Use 3 posts per shelf. This will allow the shelf to sit without a wobble. Use more posts for heavier loads, especially on the very bottom.
4. Place posts directly above posts with at least 3 per half shelf.
5. Keep lower shelves several inches apart, as close spacing can cause the kiln to fire more slowly.
6. Leave room around the thermocouple and kiln sitter (1-2" from shelves and wares).
7. Items to be bisque-fired can touch and/or be stacked.
8. Items to be glaze-fired should not touch each other or posts and be spaced 1-2" apart.
9. Wipe off the bottom wiped off of glazed items or rest them on a star or other stilt.
10. To conserve space, put items of similar height on the same shelf.
11. It is usually best to put the tallest pieces on top, so very tall posts are not needed.
12. There should be a 1/2" space between the tallest piece and the kiln lid when closed so nothing is damaged when closing the lid.
13. Load pottery on the shelves with taller things in the center of the shelves and shorter things on the edges. This allows the radiant heat to reach the wares in the center of the shelf.
14. Remember to add your witness cones while loading. If you plan to use the cones to determine when to turn off the kiln, make sure they are visible through a peephole.
15. It is very useful to keep a firing log. Start your log entry by describing how you loaded the kiln (types and sizes of items in load, density of packing of items, firing schedule).

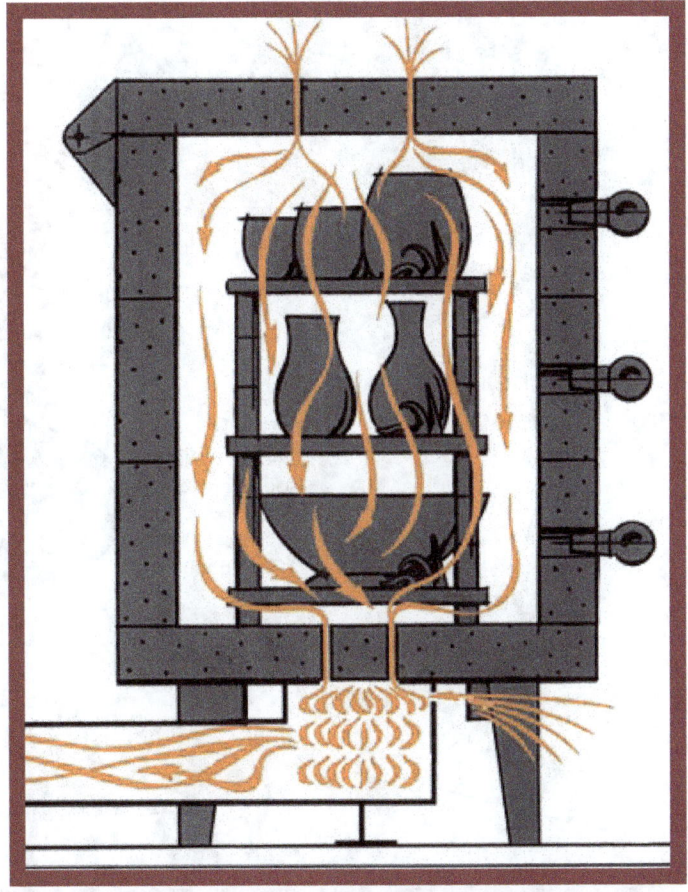

Chapter 2: Clay Tools and Equipment

Kiln Firing Chart

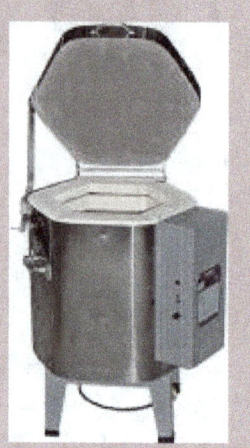

CONES:

It is very important to differentiate between Cones 06-04 and Cones 4-6, as the settings are quite different and using the wrong one could have a negative effect on the results. Cones can be used to gauge the temperature in the kiln. Below is an example of how they are set up and what happens during the firing process.

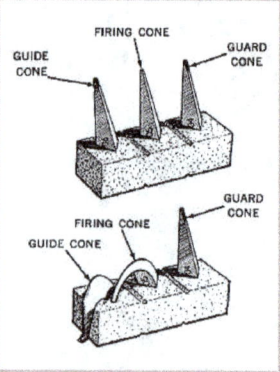

	F°	Color	C°	Cone
Very High-Fire Porcelain	2552		1400	14
	2455		1346	13
	2419		1326	12
	2399		1315	11
High-Fire Stoneware	2381		1305	10
	2336		1280	9
	2306		1263	8
	2264		1240	7
Mid-Fire Stoneware	2232		1222	6
	2185		1196	5
	2157		1186	4
	2134		1168	3
	2124		1162	2
	2109		1154	1
	2079		1137	01
	2048		1120	02
	2014		1101	03
Low-Fire Earthenware	1940		1060	04
	1915		1046	05
	1830		999	06
	1803		984	07
	1751		955	08
	1693		923	09
	1652		900	010
	1641		894	011
	1623		884	012
	1565		852	013
	1540		838	014
	1479		804	015
	1457		792	016
	1376		747	017
	1322		717	018
	1261		683	019
	1175		635	020
	1137		614	021
	1112		600	022
	900		500	
	750		400	
	550		300	
	400		200	
	212		100	

Note: Temperature equivalents are based on a rate of climb of 270°F (150°C) per hour.

Kiln Color

- High-fire glazes commonly fire at Cone 8-10. Oxidations occurs in an electric cone at Cone 10
- Mid-fire glazes commonly fire at Cone 4-6 and this is the max temperature for most commercial underglazes
- Raku clay is usually bisque-fired to cone 04-1
- Low-fire glazes commonly fire at Cone 06-04
- Bisque-firings are done at Cone 06-04 for most types of clay
- Sintering happens at 1400°F to 1650°F (800°C to 900°C), which is the stage where clay particles begin to cement themselves together creating a hard material called bisque
- Lusters and specialty glazes commonly fire at Cone 022-017
- Chemically combines water is driven off between 900°F to 1200°F (480°C to 700°C)
- Quartz inversion: During a glaze firing the crystals change their structure at 1063°F (573°C)
- Kitchen oven max temperature is 550°F (285°C)
- Vegetable matter and paper burn off as smoke at 390°F (200°C)
- Water boils and converts to steam at 212°F (100°C). Trapped water will cause clay to explode, so drying below 200°F (95°C)

GLASS FUSING in the KILN

A ceramic kiln can be used to fuse glass.
Full Fuse: 1480°F (805°C) **Tack Fuse:** 1350°F (730°C)
Slumping: 1220°F (665°C)
Note: Following a detailed firing schedule for each type of fusing is necessary for desired results.

Clay Methods Vocabulary

Terms for Wedging, Coil, Slab, Pinch and other Clay Methods

Chapter 3 Clay Methods Vocabulary

Wedging Clay Terms

What is Wedging?

Wedging is kneading/pressing clay to remove air bubbles and even out clay consistency.

Wedging Methods

Rams (Bull) Head Method: This popular method has two hands both doing the same actions of pushing and pulling the clay to form a ram's head-like symmetrical form.

Spiral (Shell) Method: This method has each hand doing different motions and results in an asymmetrical shell-like form.

Stack and Slam Method: Repetitively stacking, slamming and slicing through blocks of clay.

Spanking Method (Modified Wedging): This simple technique is done by 'spanking' and rotating clay. Mostly helps with shaping the clay.

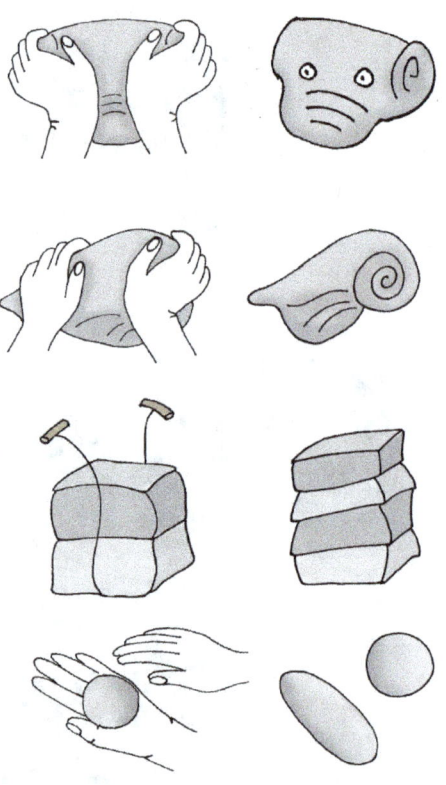

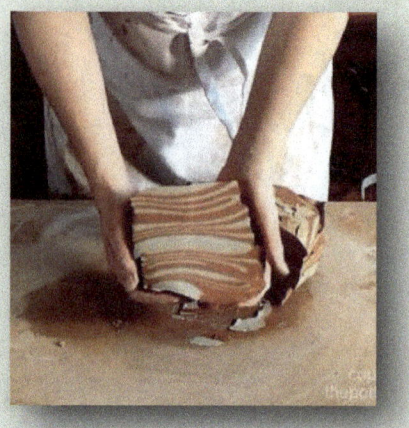

Why Wedge?

Wedging
- makes clay more pliable
- ensures a uniform consistency
- removes air pockets and any hard spots in the clay.

Wedging clay is a great way to make clay into
- a ball for working on the wheel or making a pinch pot
- a 'loaf' for putting it in the slab roller.

www.artboxadventures.net   artboxadventures@gmail.com

Chapter 3 Clay Methods Vocabulary

Clay Forming Methods

Ways to Construct/Create with Clay

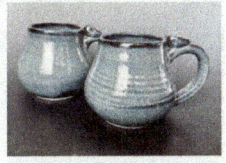	**Wheel Throwing**	Using a pottery wheel to make functional or sculptural ceramic pieces
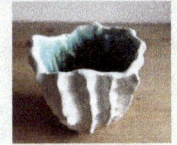	**Pinch**	Using thumb and fingers to press a ball of clay into a hollow form
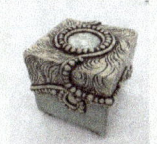	**Slab**	Rolling flat pieces of clay, usually with a rolling pin or slab roller
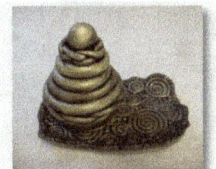	**Coil**	Rolling clay into long, thin, snake-like rolls that can be cut, folded, spiraled and twisted
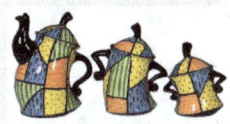	**Extruding**	Creating long, solid and hollow clay forms with an extruder
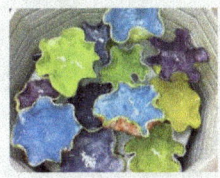	**Slumping & Draping**	Bending a slab of clay on top of or inside of a mold
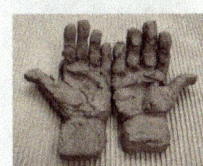	**Modeling/ Sculpting**	Shaping clay with hands and simple tools; refined with additive and/or subtractive details
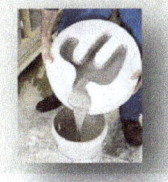	**Slip Casting**	Using liquid clay and molds to create ceramic forms

Consider Combining Techniques for Creative Results

www.artboxadventures.net   artboxadventures@gmail.com

Chapter 3 Clay Methods Vocabulary

Wheel Throwing Terms

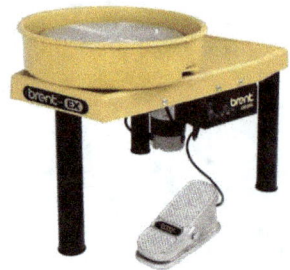

Wheel Throwing
Forming clay on a potter's wheel

Bat: A base for throwing, hand-building, or drying, usually made of plastic, wood or plaster.

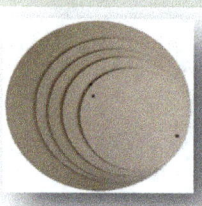

Coning: Squeezing the clay upward into a cone-like shape as a step to centering the clay on the wheel.

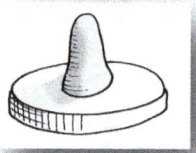

Centering: The process of applying pressure to a lump of clay on a spinning wheel to position it for even rotation.

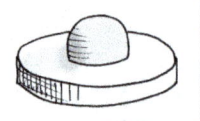

Opening: Making a hollow cavity in the centered clay.

Potter's/Pottery Wheel: A device with a manual (foot powered) or electric rotating wheel head used to make pottery.

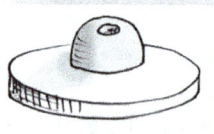

Pulling: Making the walls taller by using gentle pressure on the spinning clay.

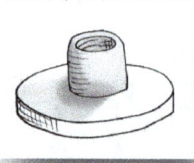

Shaping: Alter the shape of a piece to give it the desired look or function.

Splash Pan: A molded plastic tray placed around the potter's wheel to keep clay and water from spraying on the potter or onto the floor.

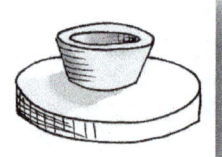

Trimming: Refining the shape and base of leather-hard clay using carving tools.

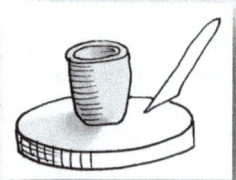

Wheel Head: The flat, circular, metal spinning surface upon which the pot is formed.

Why is it called Throwing?
The term "to throw" comes from the Old English word *thrawan*, which means to turn, twist or propel.

Wheel Throwing Tools
Commonly used tools include needle tool, loop tool, ribbon tool, potter's rib, wire clay cutter, metal scraper, wood modeling/trimming tool, and sponge.

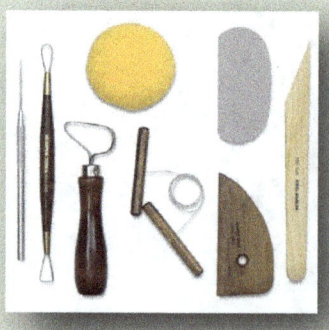

www.artboxadventures.net — artboxadventures@gmail.com

Chapter 3 Clay Methods Vocabulary

Pinch Pot Terms

Pinch Pot
A technique used to create a small bowl-like forms using a pinching motion.

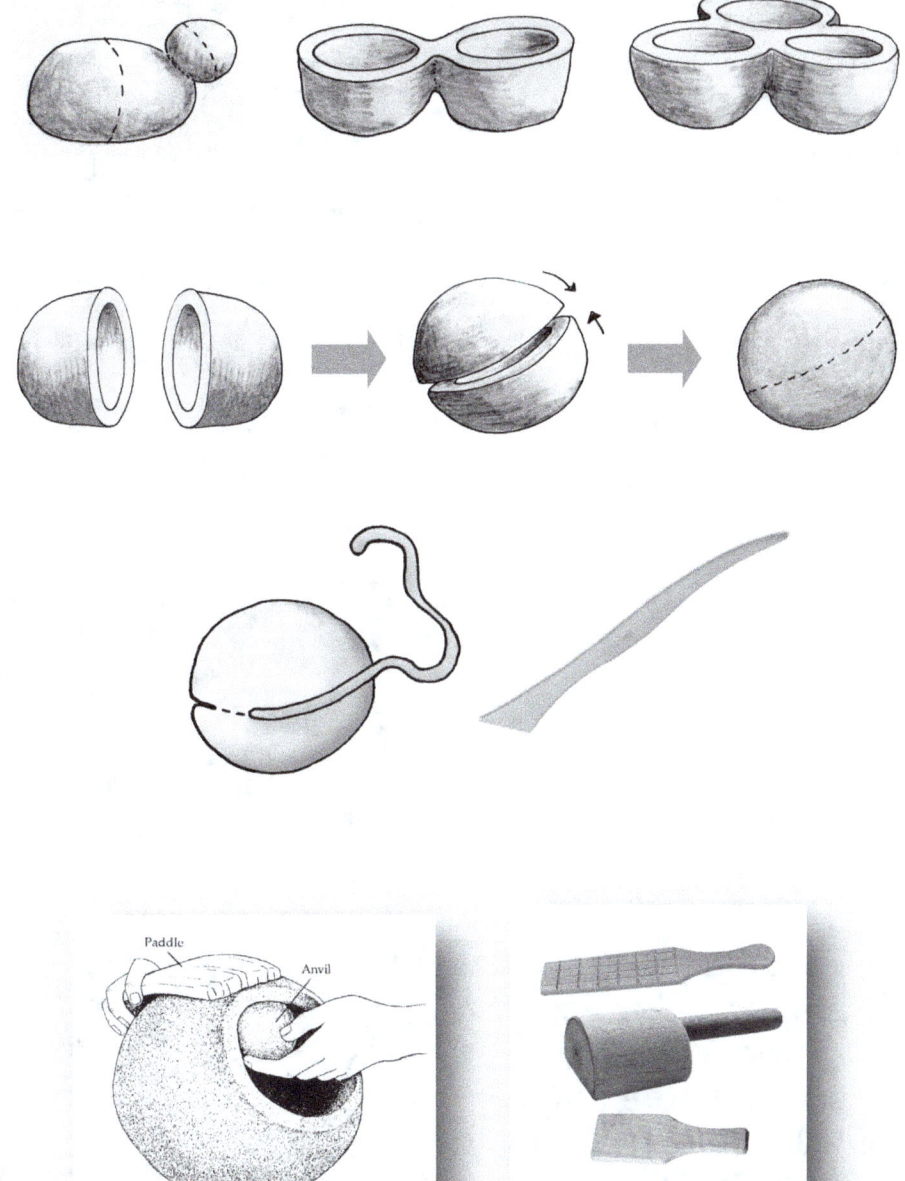

Connected Pinch Pots
When two or more pinch pots are joined.

Double Pinch Pot
When connecting two pinch pots the same size to create a hollow sphere.

'Scarf' or 'Band-Aid' Technique
When creating double pinch pots, wrap a narrow coil around the seam like a scarf or band-aid and then blend it in.
This helps get rid of the indent and make the join stronger.

Paddling
Shape clay by gently hitting with a wooden paddle to removed dents and achieve the form you want.

Chapter 3 Clay Methods Vocabulary

Coiling Terms

Coiling

Coil Construction or coiling involves the forming and joining of narrow snake-like coils of clay to create the walls of a vessel or sculpture.

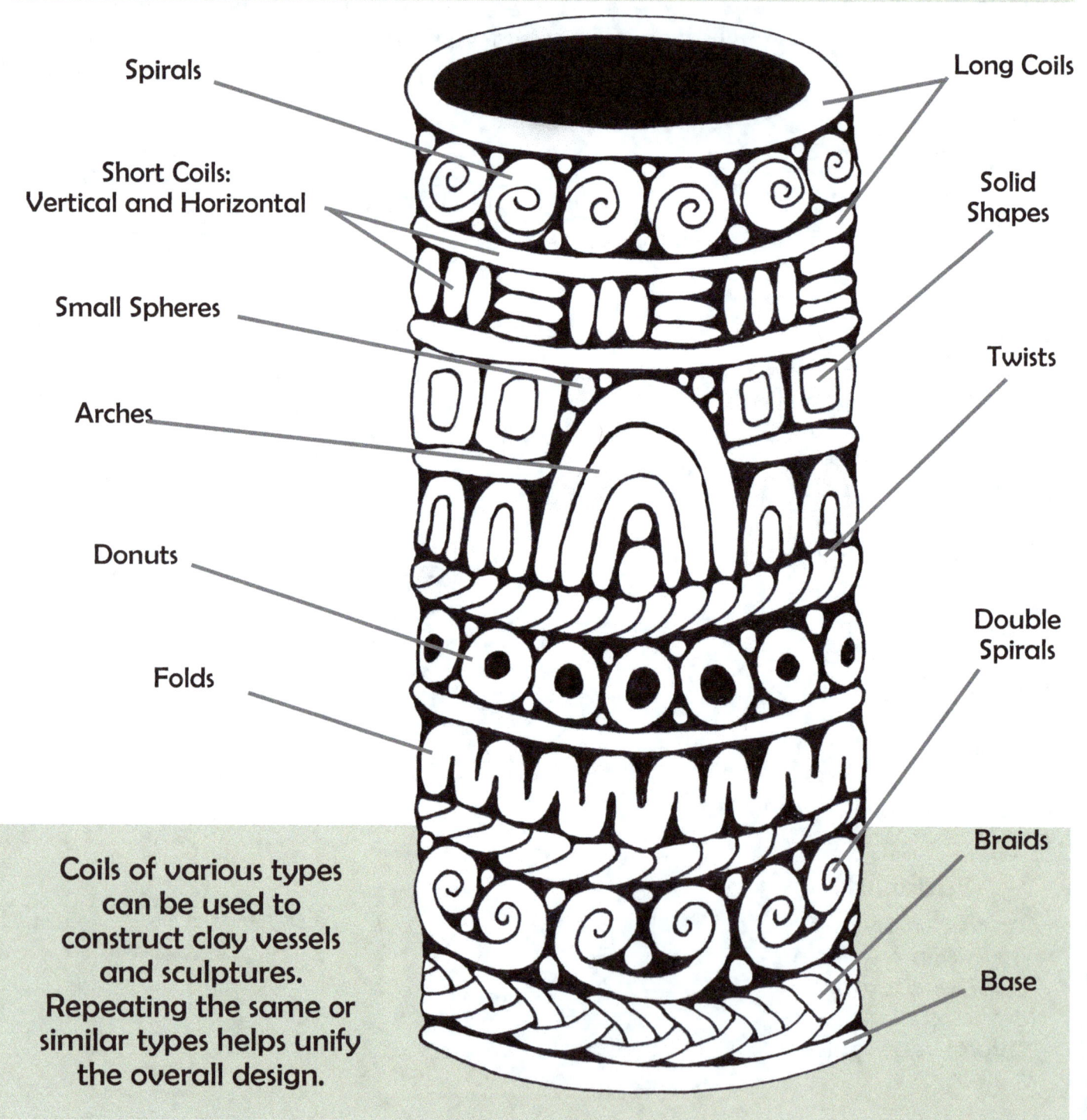

- Spirals
- Short Coils: Vertical and Horizontal
- Small Spheres
- Arches
- Donuts
- Folds
- Long Coils
- Solid Shapes
- Twists
- Double Spirals
- Braids
- Base

Coils of various types can be used to construct clay vessels and sculptures. Repeating the same or similar types helps unify the overall design.

www.artboxadventures.net   artboxadventures@gmail.com

Chapter 3 Clay Methods Vocabulary

Types of Coils

Spirals	Arches
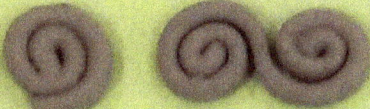	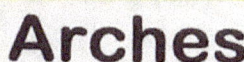
Short Coils	Donuts
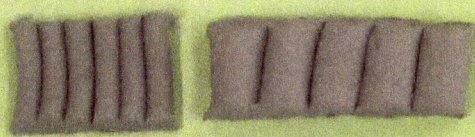	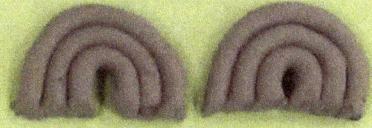
Long Coils	Folds
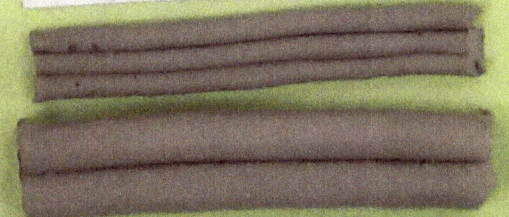	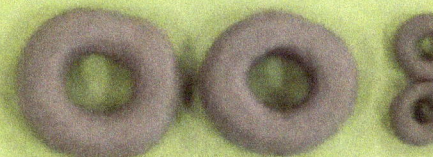
Twists	Spheres
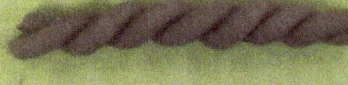	Small Half Flattened
Braids	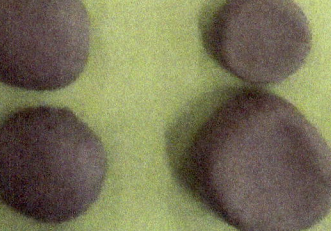

www.artboxadventures.net   artboxadventures@gmail.com

Chapter 3 Clay Methods Vocabulary

Slabs Method Terms

Slab
A slab is a piece of clay which has been made flat, usually by rolling with a rolling pin or slab roller.

Slabs can be used in a variety of ways including **Slab Construction** (Soft Slab and Hard Slab) and **Flat Slab Creations** (Relief Slab or Slab Sculpture Base)

Slab Construction

Slab construction is a hand-building technique in which flat pieces of clay are joined together.

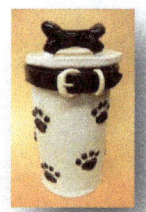
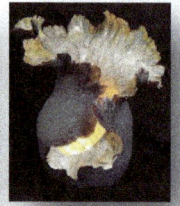

Soft Slab Construction: Forms constructed while clay is in the wet/plastic stage so that the slabs can be curved, bent or folded to make curved sculptural or functional artworks.

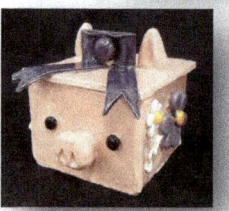
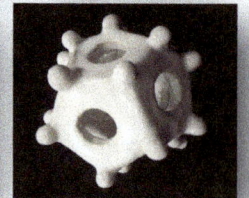

Hard Slab Construction: Slabs are rolled and then allowed to slowly dry to the leather-hard stage before being cut and joined to create sculptural or functional artworks with flat sides.

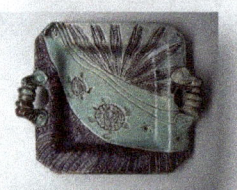
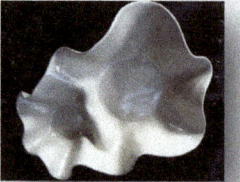

Flat Slab Creations

Slumped or Draped Slabs: Clay is laid within the mold or draped over top.

Relief Slab Sculpture: Sculptural elements are carved into or attached to a slab, such as a tile.

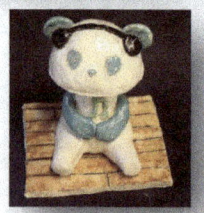
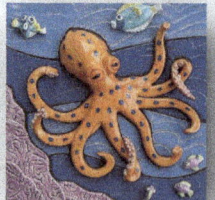

Slab Sculpture Base: Slabs are used as bases for sculptures to provide additional support.

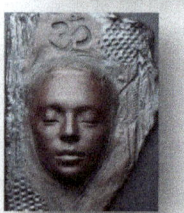
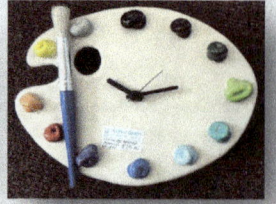

www.artboxadventures.net   artboxadventures@gmail.com

Chapter 3 Clay Methods Vocabulary

Extruding Terms

Extrude
"The act or process of shaping by forcing through a die."

Extruder
Barrel shaped equipment used to make coils of assorted shapes and sizes.

Note: Extruders can also extrude hollow forms.

What can you do with an extruder?

Extruders are great for making coils for coil construction or coil decorating, handles and hollow forms.

Dies vary in size and shape. Hollow forms require a die holder (spider) to create a donut-like hole to extrude clay.

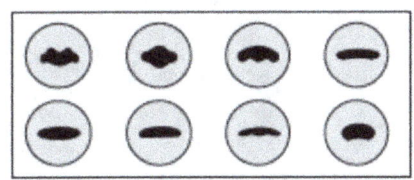
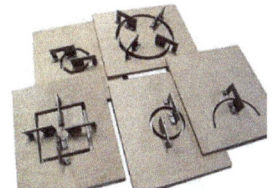

Dies and Die-Holders

Coiling
Constructing, decorating and sculpting with coils

Handles
Making handles to attach to functional vessels

Hollow Forms
Extruded hollow functional and sculptural forms

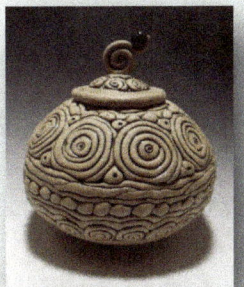
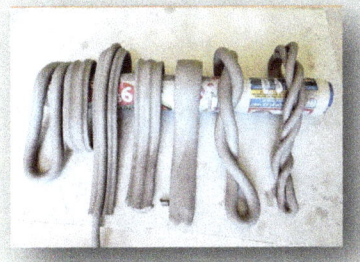
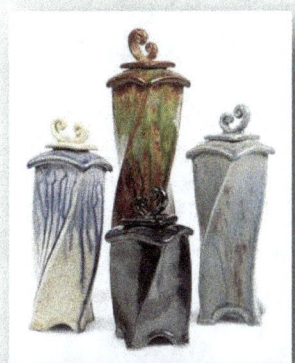
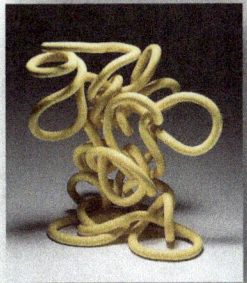
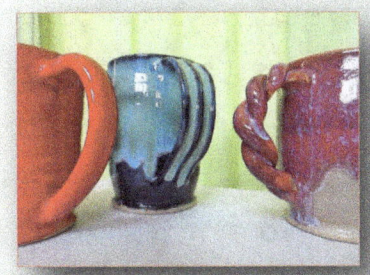
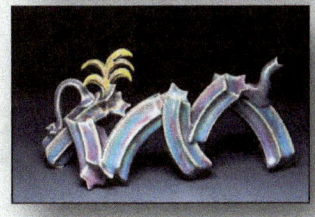

www.artboxadventures.net · artboxadventures@gmail.com

Chapter 3 Clay Methods Vocabulary

Slump & Drape Mold Terms

Slabs can be used to create functional and sculptural artworks using slumping and draping techniques

Concave
Hollowed or rounded inward, curving away like the inside of a bowl.

Convex
Having a surface or boundary that curves or bulges outward, like an upside-down bowl.

Slump
To fall or sink heavily. Collapse or droop.

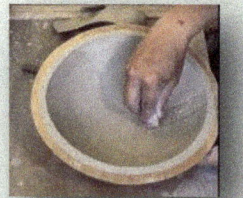

Drape
To cover, hang, let fall or rest limply in loose folds.

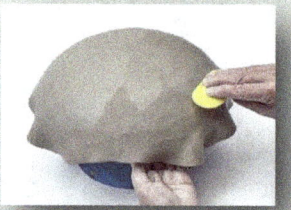

Slump Mold
A typically shallow concave frame or mold into which a slab of clay is allowed to fall or settle to form a vessel.
Open-center (donut-like) molds can also be used to allow the natural curve of the slab itself to shape the form.

Drape Mold
(also called Hump Molds)
A convex form over which a clay slab is draped until stiff enough to hold its shape. Clay can be draped loosely or pressed to exactly follow the form of the mold.

Slump or Drape Mold Materials

Molds can be made of plaster, wood, bisque-fired clay, plastic, glass, metal, foam or other materials. Nearly any object can be used, but some non-porous surfaces need plastic wrap, newspaper or paper towels sandwiched between the clay slab and the mold to keep the clay from sticking.

Porous: Wood and plaster are porous surfaces that will absorb some moisture and work well for slumping and draping clay.

Non-Porous: Materials like metal, glass or glazed pottery will not absorb water and clay tends to stick to them. Non-porous molds need to have a barrier between them and the clay.

Chapter 3 Clay Methods Vocabulary

Modeling/Sculpting Terms

Modeling

Sculpting, shaping or forming using a pliable material, such as clay.

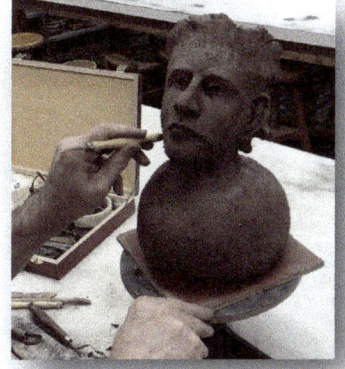

Modeling/Sculpting Methods

Manipulate Clay
Clay is Altered
Use soft, pliable clay. Start sculpting clay by molding it into the rough shape desired. This can be done by pushing, pulling, squishing and moving clay into its basic form. You can manipulate the clay with your hands or tools.

Additive
Clay is Added
Add parts to the rough form. It is often good to let the rough shape firm up a bit without becoming too dry. Use tools or fingers to add soft clay and define the shape further. The two clays should be of similar consistency to prevent cracking. If the clays vary much, scoring and slip are recommended when adding pieces.

Subtractive
Clay is Removed
Selectively taking away, removing or 'subtracting from' a piece of clay. This can be done by Carving, Scooping/Hollowing Out and Scraping. Both large and small amounts of clay can be removed.

Repositioning
Parts are Moved
If some part of your artwork doesn't look quite right, some surgery may be required. Use a knife or sharp tool to cut off whole sections and rejoin using slip and scoring.

Details
Clay Surface is Altered
Refine artwork with additional details such as textures, stamping, carving or sprig molds (see next page). Details may be additive or subtractive.

Modeling Tools
Lots of tools can be used for modeling clay, including commercially made tools, handmade tools and everyday objects.

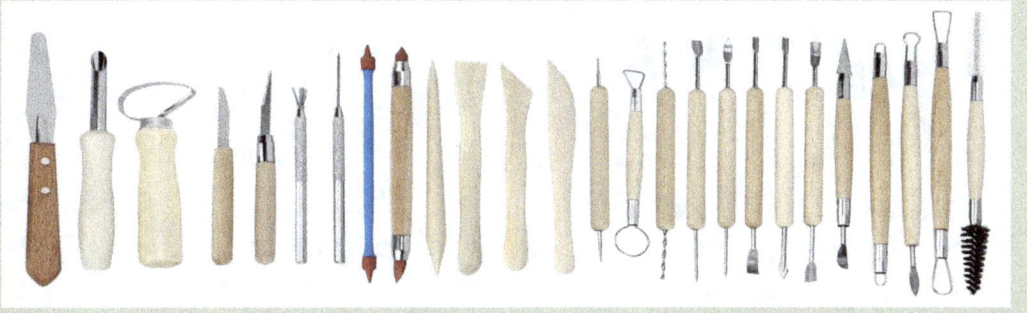

www.artboxadventures.net artboxadventures@gmail.com

Chapter 3 Clay Methods Vocabulary

Slip Casting Terms

Slip Casting

Slip or liquid clay is poured into a plaster mold. The plaster absorbs the water, allowing layers of clay to easily build up against the inside walls of the mold creating a cast piece.

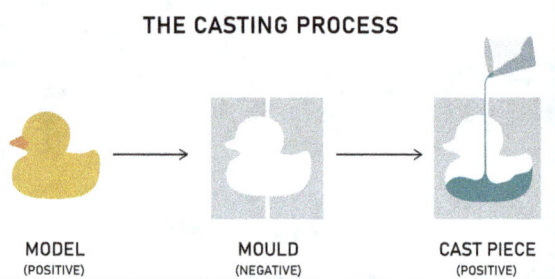

Why Use Slip Casting?

Slip casting is used to efficiently make multiple copies of ceramic sculptures and functional wares.

Types of Slip Molds

Slip Casting Supplies

Plaster Mold
Thick Rubber Bands/Straps
Slip
Stain (Optional)
Slip Mixer
Bucket
Pitcher/Jug
Wooden Spoon/Spatula
Sieve Sponge
Fettling Knife
File/Wet & Dry Sandpaper

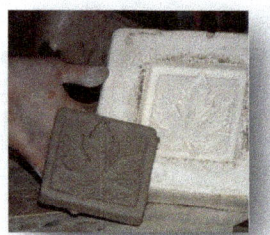

One-Piece Molds: Usually for tiles & relief sculptures

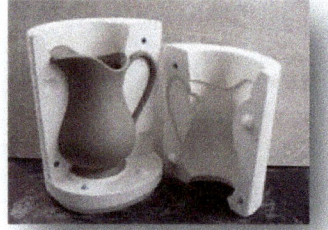

Two-Piece Molds: Used to make 3D forms

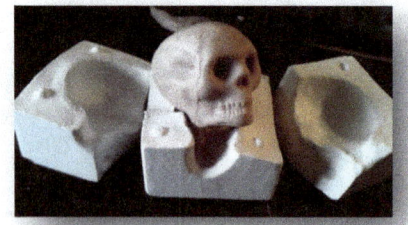

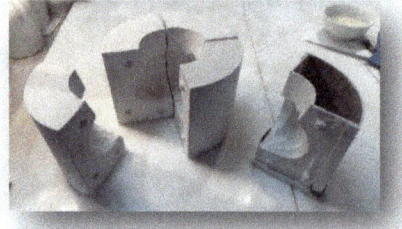

Multiple Piece Molds: Used to make complex 3D forms

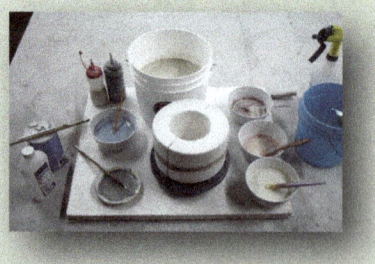

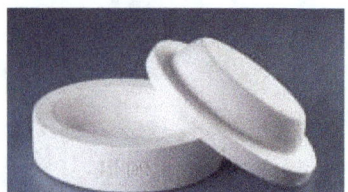

Press Molds: Clay is pressed, rather than poured into the mold

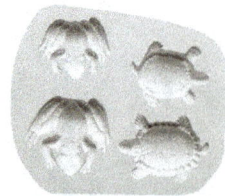

Sprig Molds: Small relief details to add onto a clay base

Tip: Use sodium silicate to thin down the slip down if it gets too thick.

www.artboxadventures.net   artboxadventures@gmail.com

Chapter 3 Clay Methods Vocabulary

Surface Decoration Terms

There are many ways to enhance or alter the surface of clay.

Incising
Carving or engraving a design in to clay by cutting or scraping into the surface

Slip Trailing
Drawing onto the surface of clay with slip using a fine-tipped dispenser

Excising
Carving away the background around an image/shape on the surface of the clay, leaving a raised relief image

Faceting
Cutting away strips of a pot's surface with knives, razors or coiled wire tools

Impressing
Stamping or embossing textures or designs with an object, tool or stamp or scraping into the surface

Fluting
Using a carving tool to extract ribbons of clay leaving a trough-like appearance on the surface of the piece

Sgraffito
Carving a clay surface, through layers of underglaze or colored slip, to leave behind an incised image or design

Combing
Making parallel lines on the surface of a pot with a tool or hand

Piercing
Cutting shapes, letters or designs through the wall of a pot while in the leather-hard state

Wax Resist
Brushing a wax medium over an area of clay, slip, or glaze to resist the final glaze application

Sprigging
Decorating pottery with low relief shapes with forms are usually made separately using a mold and then applied before firing

Stenciling
Cutting or tearing paper shapes, adhering them to leather-hard clay and then applying slip/glaze over the clay surface

Burnishing
Rubbing the surface of leather-hard clay with a hard object to create a smooth, glossy surface

Brushwork
Painting with a brush in a loose or precise manner to give different effects

Mishima
Filling an incised design/lines with colored slip or underglaze

Sponging
Using a sponge to apply glaze or underglaze to create gradients of color

Image Transfer
Applying photographic or drawn images to clay as templates, prints, stencils or decals

Drawing on Clay
Drawing on clay with ceramic pencil or underglaze pen

Chapter 3 Clay Methods Vocabulary

Glazing and Other Common Finishing Method Terms

Ways to add color to the surface of bisque-fired clay

Glaze

Glaze is the most common way to add color and finish clay artworks. It is applied to bisqueware and can be clear or colored.

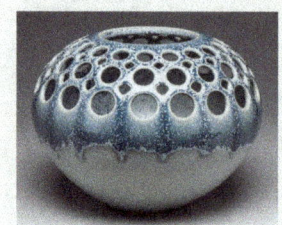

Underglaze

Underglazes can be applied to Greenware (unfired clay) or Bisqueware. May be coated with clear glaze to seal it or give it a shiny finish.

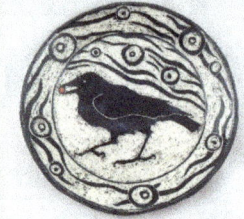

Stains & Oxides

Stains and oxides can be applied to bisqueware and then wiped to emphasize texture. To seal and add shine, apply clear glass over top.

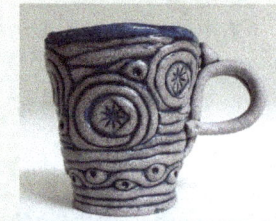

Lusters

Lusters are overglazes applied on glaze-fired pieces and require a third firing. Lusters are often metallic and fired at a lower temperature.

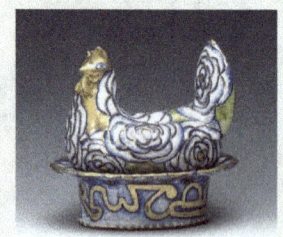

Paint

Paint, including acrylic, watercolor or tempera, can be applied on bisque-fired clay. Paint is used mostly on ceramic sculptures.

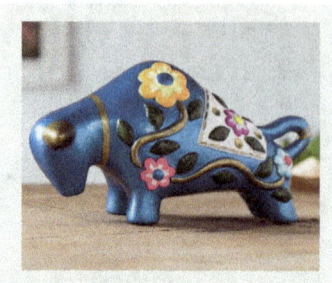

Sculptural & Functional Clay Terms

Chapter 4 Sculptural & Functional Clay Terms

Terms Related to
Form & Function

Ceramic artworks can be functional, sculptural or both.

Here are some terms that are helpful in discussing or thinking about the functional and sculptural qualities of a clay artwork.

Aesthetics: The study or theory of "beauty" and of the psychological responses to it.

Decorative: Serving to decorate, ornamental, designed to look pretty.

Design: The relationship between the parts of a ceramic piece.

Form: The aesthetic appeal of an object.

Function: An object's purpose or intent

Functional: An object that has a specified purpose for which it is designed.

Functionality: The degree of practicality in actually using an object.

Form: The way in which parts of a whole are organized.

Sculptural: Relating to or having three-dimensional qualities.

Sculpture: The art or practice of shaping figures or designs in the round or in relief, as by carving, modeling, assembling or casting.

Utilitarian: When a piece's function is much more important than its form.

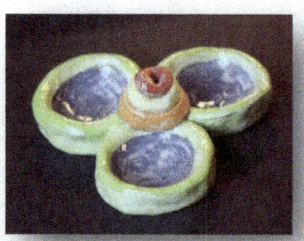
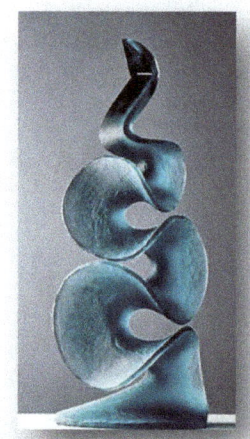
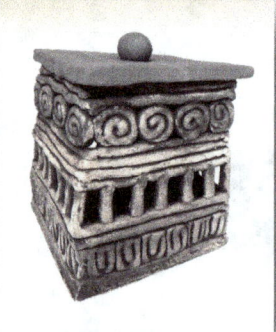
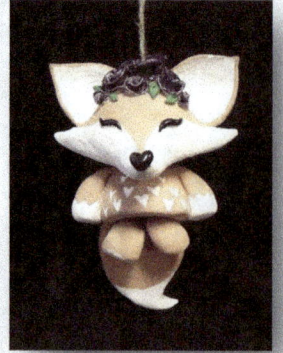
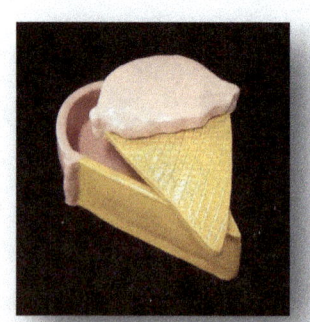
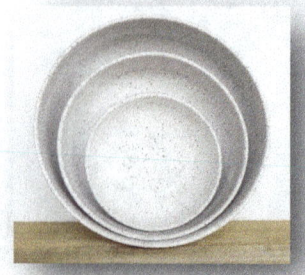
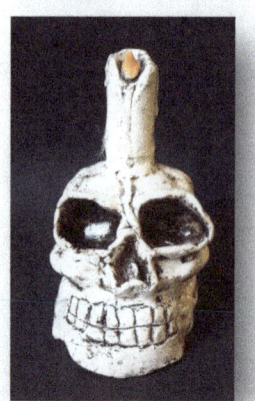

www.artboxadventures.net   artboxadventures@gmail.com

Clay Sculpture Terms

Types of Clay Sculpture

Sculptures In-the-Round are generally designed to be viewed from multiple angles and are free-standing.

Relief Sculptures have sculptural elements carved into or attached on to a flat surface. They are generally meant to be viewed from one side only.

Additive Sculptures are created by adding clay to a form or base.

Subtractive Sculptures are created by removing unwanted clay to create the form.

Kinetic or Mobile Sculptures have movable parts. Ceramic sculptures may include other materials such as wire, bead, string or cord.

What is Sculpture?

Sculpture is the creation of expressive forms in three dimensions.

Sculpture is the art of making three-dimensional representative or abstract forms.

Sculptures are made of materials that have mass and exists in three-dimensional space.

4 Ways to Create Clay Sculptures

1. **Modeling:** Artists use soft clay and slowly work on the object until they attain the desired sculptural form. Modeling often uses a combination of additive and subtractive steps as they push, pull, pinch the clay into place.
2. **Casting**: Artists add liquid clay into a mold and allows it to harden. Molds are usually made of plaster because once the clay solidifies it is easy to remove.
3. **Carving:** Artists cut away clay to achieve the design. They use the subtractive process to remove clay from a clay surface.
4. **Assembling/Constructing:** Artists gather and use found and manufactured objects in combination with clay to create mixed-media sculptures.

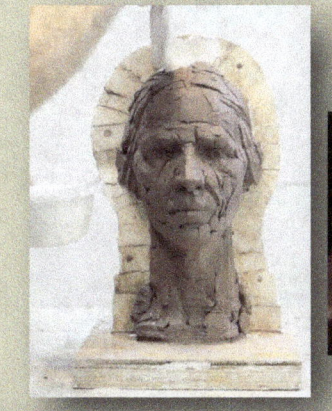
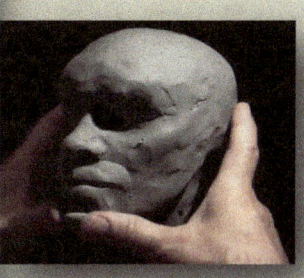
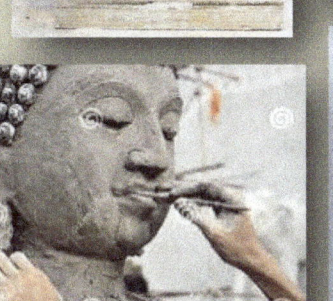
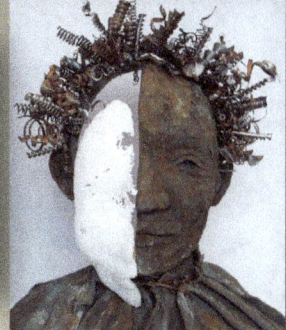

Relief Sculpture Terms

The term Relief is from the Latin verb *Relevo*, meaning to raise.

Relief sculptures and relief designs have sculptural elements carved into or attached on to a surface. This could be a 2D surface such as a tile or could on a 3D surface such as on the side of a vase.

Types of Relief Sculptures

1. **Low Relief:** (Basso-Relievo or Bas-Relief, where the sculptural designs projects only slightly from the background surface.

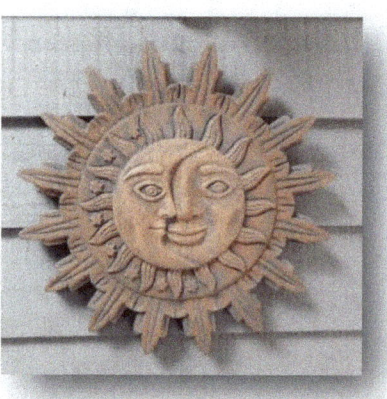

2. **High Relief:** (Alto-Relievo or Alto-Relief), where the sculptural design projects at least half its thickness from the background.

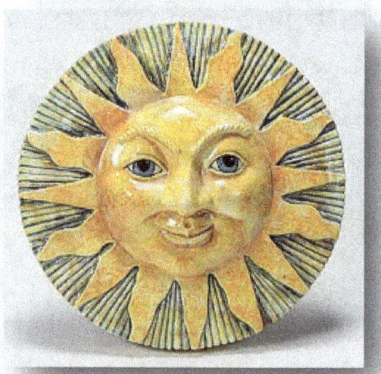

3. **Sunken Relief:** (Incised, intaglio), where the carving is sunk below the level of the background surface.

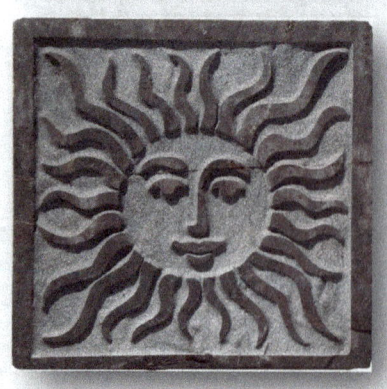

Artists may also employ middle-relief (Mezzo-Relievo), a style which falls roughly between the high and low form.

WHAT IS A VESSEL?

A hollow container, especially one used to hold liquid.

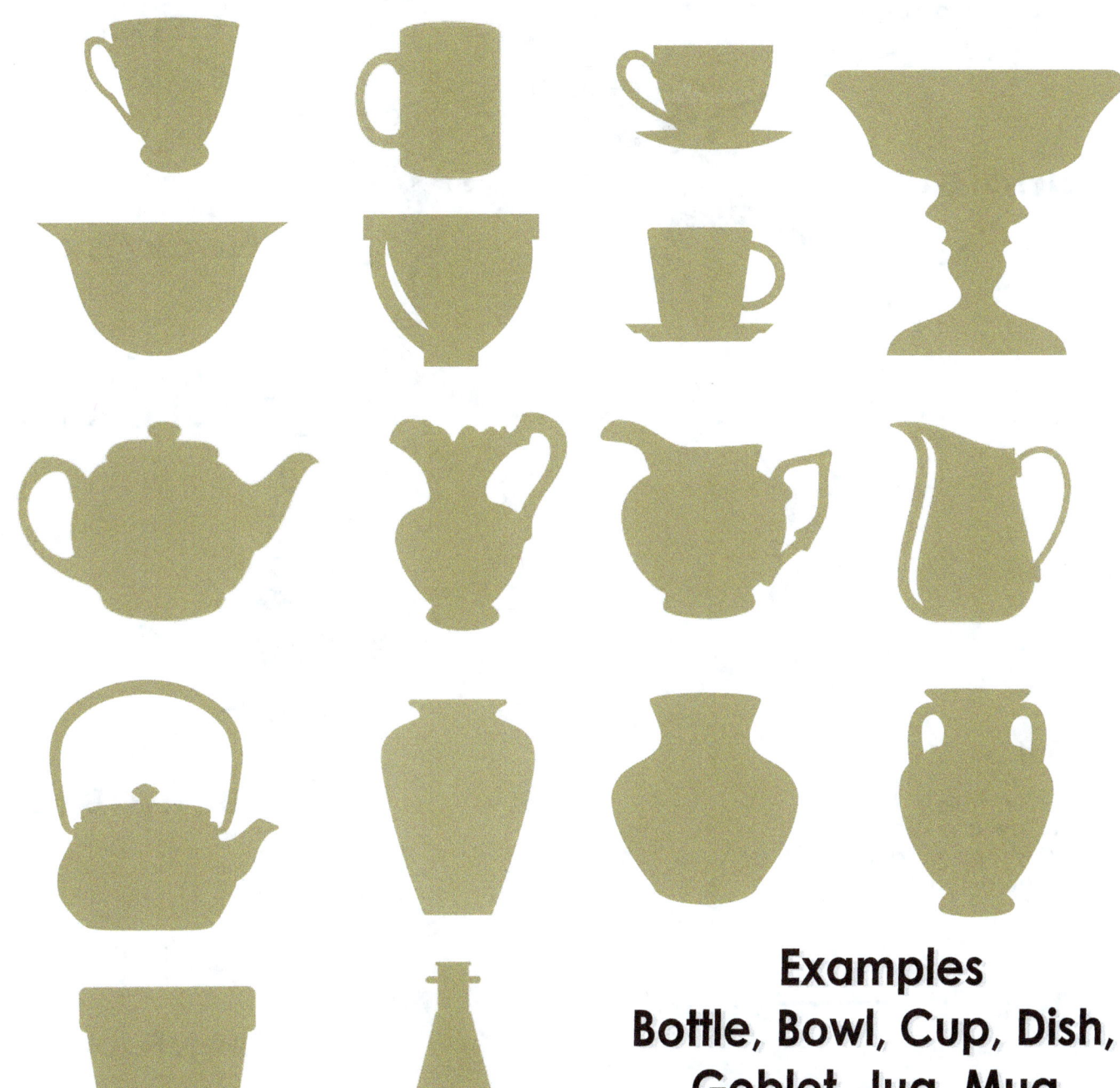

Examples
Bottle, Bowl, Cup, Dish, Goblet, Jug, Mug, Pitcher, Tea Pot or Vase

Chapter 4 Sculptural & Functional Clay Terms

Anatomy Of A
VESSEL

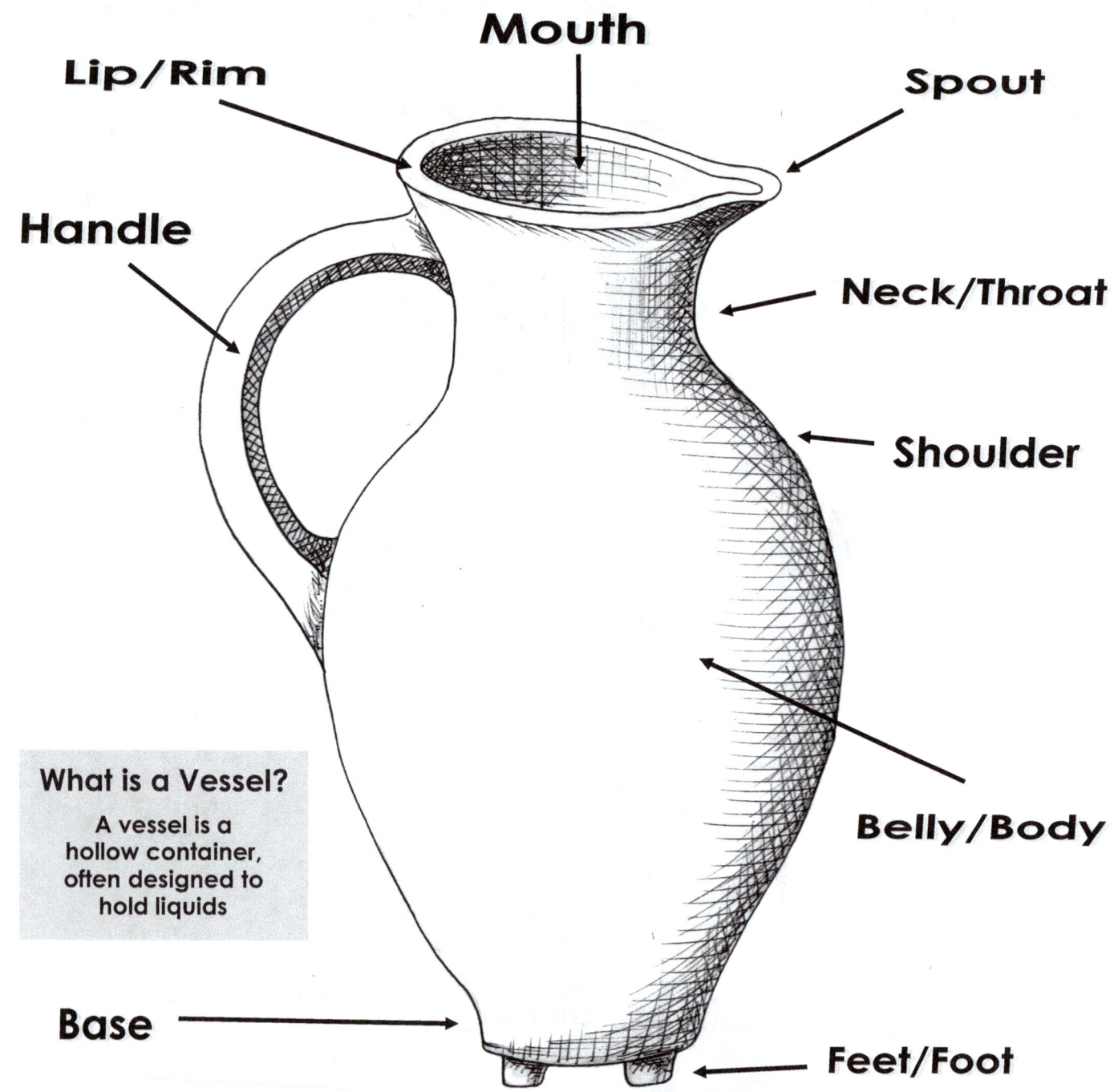

- Mouth
- Lip/Rim
- Spout
- Handle
- Neck/Throat
- Shoulder
- Belly/Body
- Base
- Feet/Foot

What is a Vessel?
A vessel is a hollow container, often designed to hold liquids

BOTTLE · BOWL · CUP · DISH · JAR · JUG · MUG · PITCHER · POT · VASE

Chapter 4 Sculptural & Functional Clay Terms

Geometric Vessel Terms

Slabs can be used to create a wide variety of geometric forms. These can be used to create containers of various types. Geometric slab forms can also be used to create sculptural pieces.

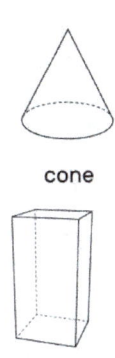
cone

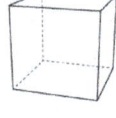
cube

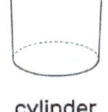
cylinder

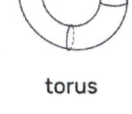
dodecahedron

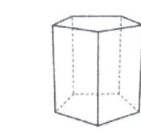
torus

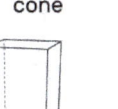
cuboid

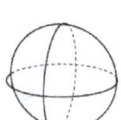
sphere

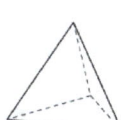
tetrahedron

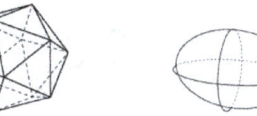
icosahedron

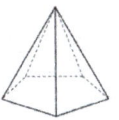
ellipsoid

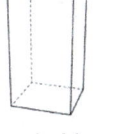
hexagonal pyramid

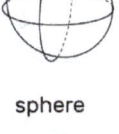
triangular prism

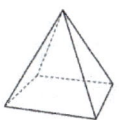
square pyramid

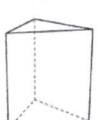
octahedron

pentagonal prism

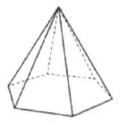
hemisphere

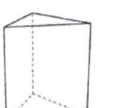
hexagonal prism

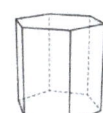
parallelepiped

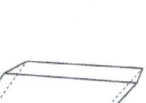
pentagonal pyramid

Planes & Slabs

When looking at geometric forms with flat sides, you can see the different planes used to construct the form.

Plane

A two-dimensional surface has height and width.

Planes can be used to define edges, or to change the 'flow' of a sculpture.

Paper Templates

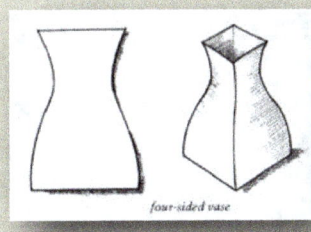
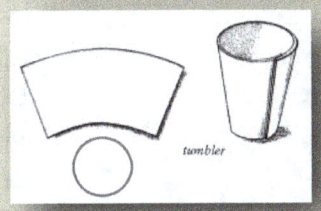

Paper Templates are a great strategy to use when constructing geometric clay forms. There are plenty of templates available online that can be printed to the size you want. Some versions have the multiple connected sides (see right), while other templates require separate pieces (see left).

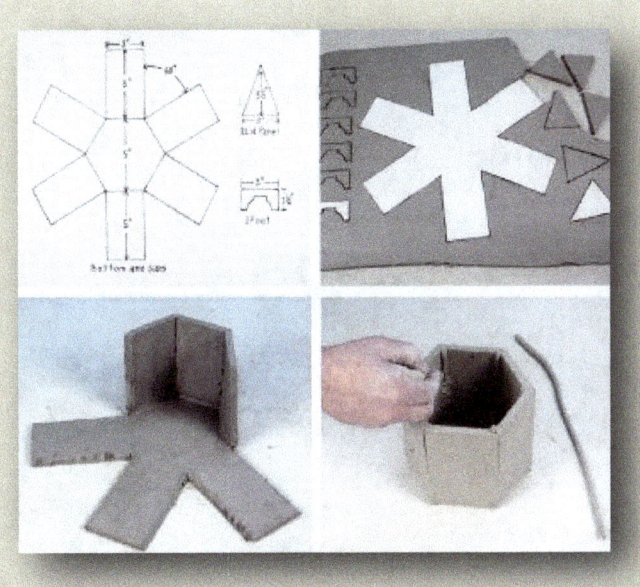

www.artboxadventures.net   artboxadventures@gmail.com

Chapter 4 Sculptural & Functional Clay Terms

Curved Geometric Vessel Terms

Vessels with curved sides can be classified by their basic geometric forms and by their type of opening.

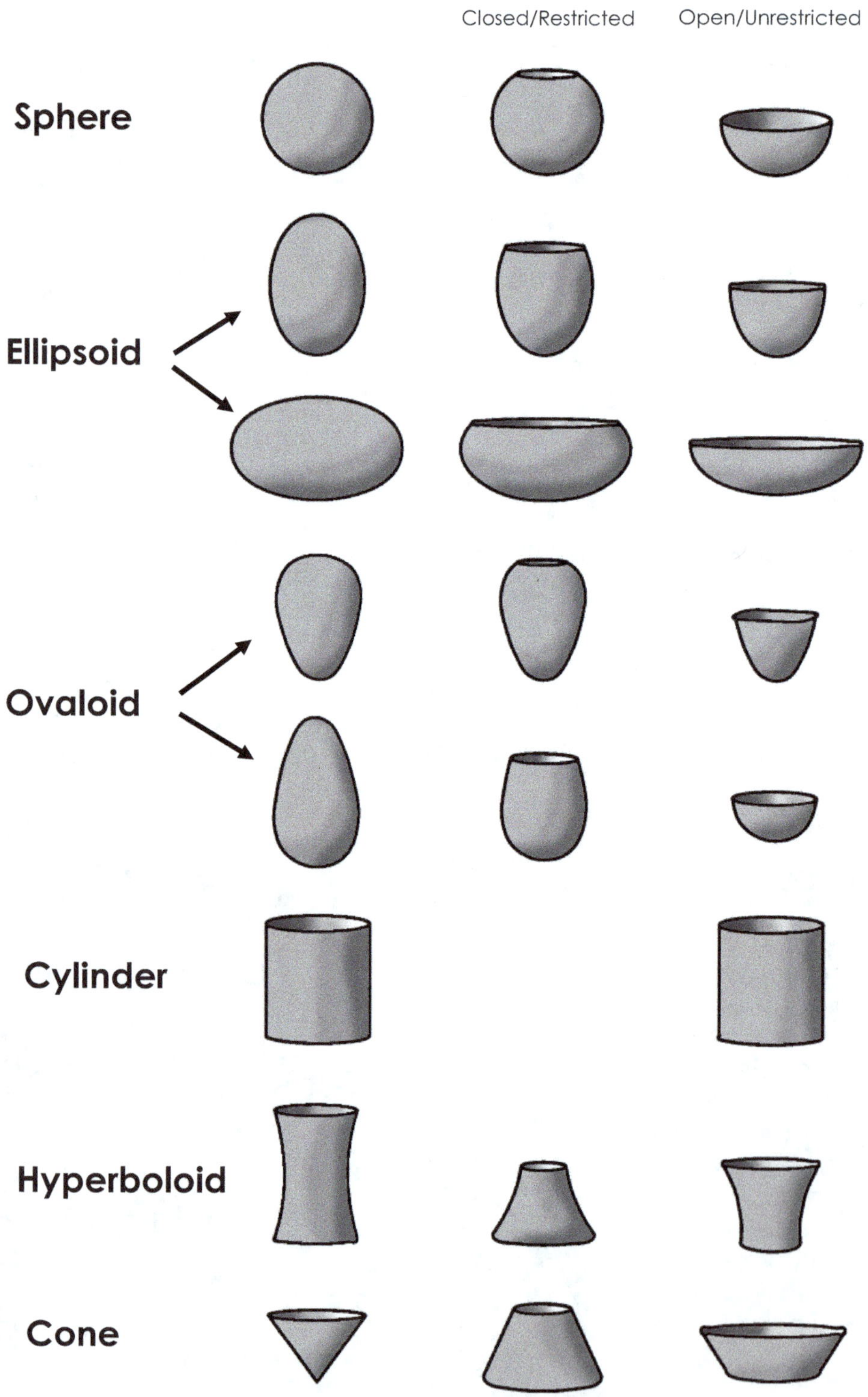

	Closed/Restricted	Open/Unrestricted
Sphere		
Ellipsoid		
Ovaloid		
Cylinder		
Hyperboloid		
Cone		

Classifying Forms Open Vs Closed

OPEN: 'Open' or unrestricted forms have a mouth opening diameter equal or greater than the maximum diameter of the body.

CLOSED: For 'closed' or restricted forms, the diameter of the body of the pot narrows between its maximum diameter and its opening.

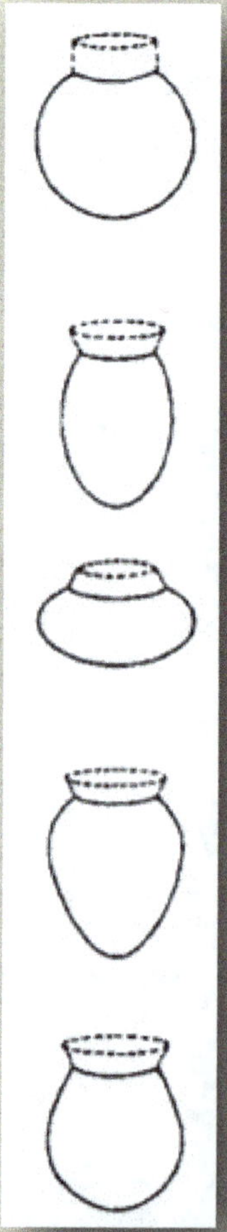

COMBO: On vessels, especially ones with bases that narrow near the top, a potter may add an extension. This adds visual interest and may alter the type of the opening.

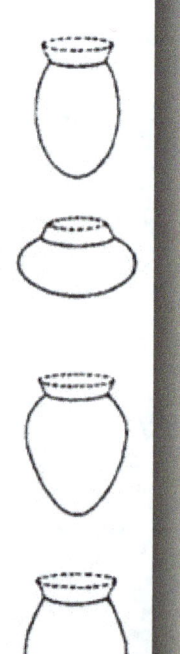

www.artboxadventures.net artboxadventures@gmail.com

Elements & Principles of Ceramic Design

Insights and Design Considerations for Clay

Chapter 5 Clay Elements & Principles of Ceramic Design

Elements of Design

ELEMENTS OF DESIGN FOR CLAY SCULPTURE

The elements are like the ingredients for a recipe to design functional and sculptural ceramics.

Line: Lines are two-dimensional, and are used in sculpture to lead the viewer's eye in, around and through a form. Can be actual or implied. They can vary in many ways including thickness, length, curvature and direction.

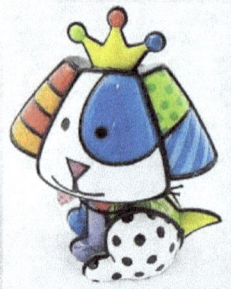

Shape: Shapes are two-dimensional and may be used on surface designs or be evident in the silhouette of a sculpture. Slabs look like shapes, but are actually forms with very little depth. Three-dimensional forms contain points (vertices), lines (edges) and planes (surfaces).

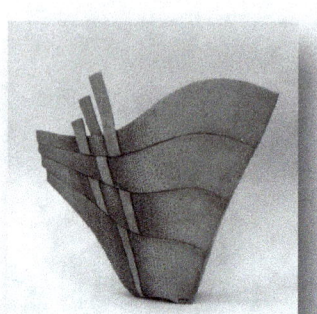

Form: A 3D sculpture has height, width and depth. Forms can be geometric or organic. Every sculpture is a form, but not every form is a sculpture.

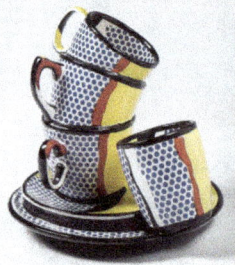

Space: Space is the height, width and depth of a 3D form. It includes the area within and around a sculpture as well.

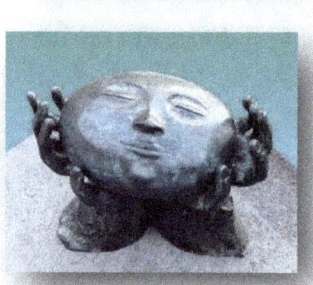

Color: Color can be used to enhance a 3D form. It can be applied (glazed or painted on) or inherent, such as the natural color of the clay. Color can be used to increase the clarity of the theme or meaning of a sculpture.

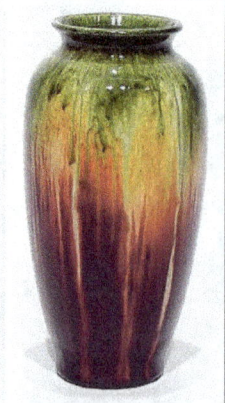

Value: Value is evident in highlights or shadows on the surface of a sculpture, meant to create interest through contrast. Textures and deeply carved areas have dark shadowed values; areas that stick out have highlighted values. Value is also evident in the lightness or darkness of glaze or paint on the surface of a sculpture.

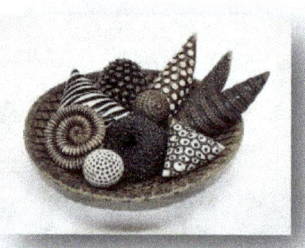

Texture: Repetitive marks a sculpture's surface create interest through contrast. Deeply textured areas appear darker and smoother; non-textured areas appear lighter.

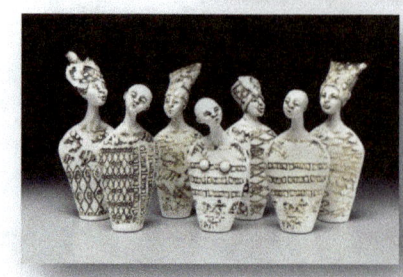

Volume and Mass; Volume is a shape in three dimensions. Mass is the density of an object (actual or perceived weight).

Chapter 5 Clay Elements & Principles of Ceramic Design

LINE

LINE

A mark with length and direction.

ASPECTS OF LINE

Line is one of the simplest elements in design. Line is a dynamic element expressing gesture or direction, activating the space that surrounds it.

In ceramics, line can be created or observed in many ways including

- Incising (carving) lines a surface
- Constructing with elongated clay pieces such as extruded or rolled coils
- Adding lines on o a surface (example adding relief coils)
- Painting lines on with glaze
- Edges of shapes or forms can create the illusion of line

Words to Describe LINE

actual
angled
blurred
broken
contour
continuous
controlled
curved
dashed
diagonal
dotted
expressive
faded
freehand
fuzzy
horizon
horizontal
implied
interrupted
meandering
overlapping
parallel
patterned
ruled
short
spiral
swirling
straight
thick
thin
vertical
wavy
wide
zig-zag

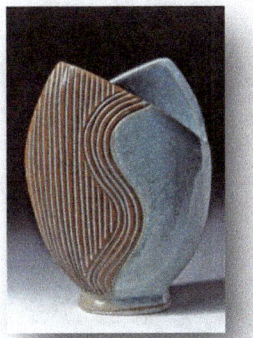
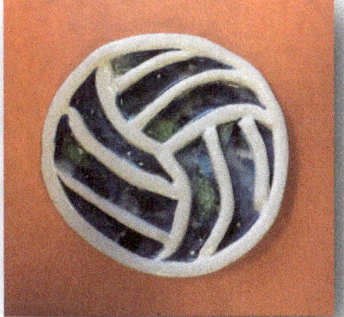
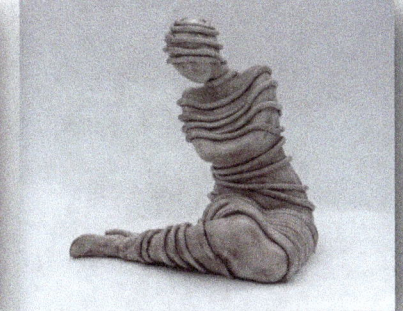
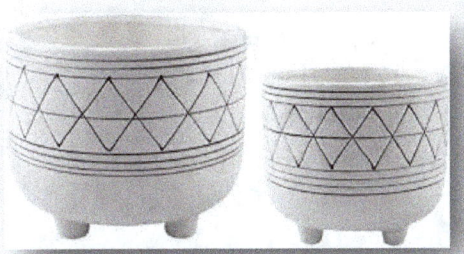
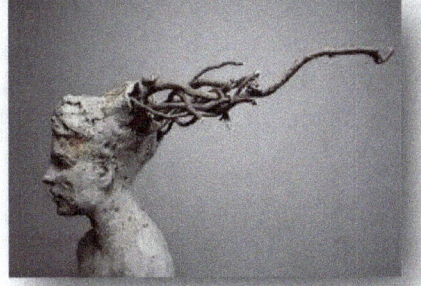

SHAPE

Words to Describe SHAPE

amorphous
angular
asymmetrical
chunky
closed
compass
concave
concentric
congruent
contorted
convoluted
convex
distorted
elliptical
flat
free form
geometric
heavy
height
isomorphic
light
linear
massive
oblong
open
organic
proportioned
round
ruler
silhouetted
simplified
symmetrical
tapered
width

SHAPE
An enclosed space, a bounded two-dimensional area that has length and width.

ASPECTS OF SHAPE

In ceramic artworks, shapes can be seen in a number of ways such as

- Slab construction
- Relief tiles/bases
- Thin slabs/shapes used for decorating
- Incised (carved) shapes
- Pierced cutouts
- Outlines made with coils or narrow slabs
- Drawn or stenciled glaze designs

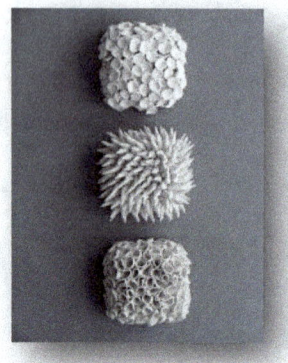
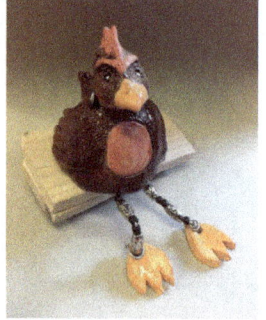
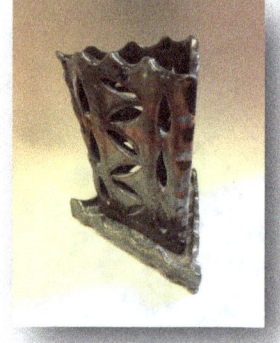
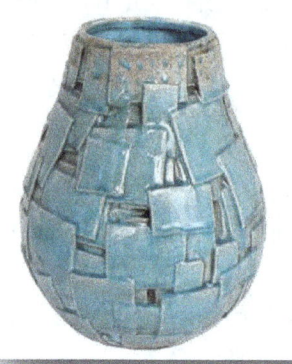
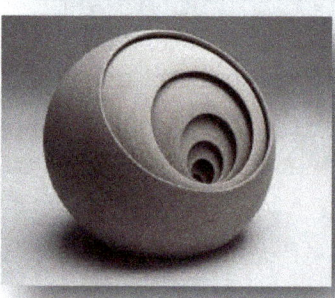
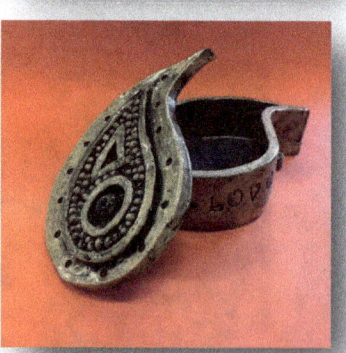
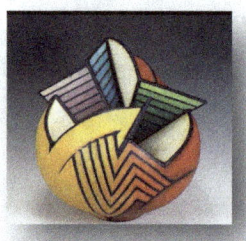
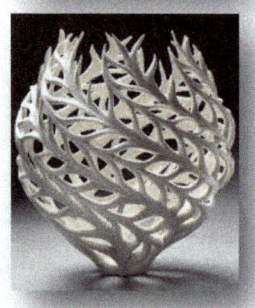

Geometric and Organic Shapes

Geometric Shapes are generally manmade, mathematical, precise, and often angular. They can often be named by their basic geometric forms: square, rectangle, triangle, hexagon, oval, etc.

Organic Shapes tend to be free-flowing and curvy. They are not usually angular, or easily measurable or named. Organic shapes are found in nature and examples include flowers, branches, leaves, puddles, clouds, animals, and the human figure.

Chapter 5 Clay Elements & Principles of Ceramic Design

FORM

FORM

A clay artwork is a form. Even relief sculptures have height, width and depth. Forms are often classified as geometric or organic.

ASPECTS OF FORM

Besides geometric and organic, forms can be classified in a number of other ways.

Static vs Dynamic

Static Forms appear to be still, stable and unchanging. They give a sense of immovable permanence.

Dynamic Forms are lively, have a sense of movement and change. They tend to have more angled planes or curved surfaces.

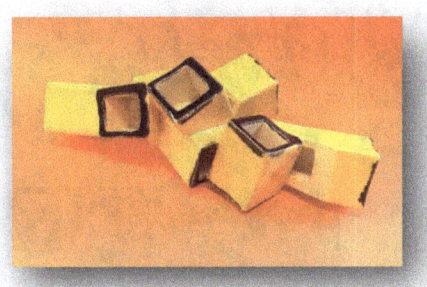 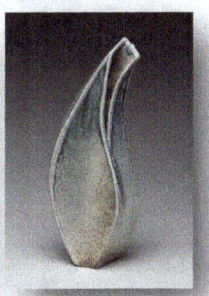

Closed vs Open

Closed Forms are solid and self-contained. They have the feel of a solid mass and generally have no or few holes or gaps.

Open Forms may have outward projections and/or holes or empty areas within them. These open spaces become a part of the artwork and often have dynamic negative spaces around and between the form.

Contours of Form

Sculptures can have interior as well as exterior contours.

- **Exterior Contours** are the visible outer surface
- **Interior Contours** are created by contours or curves in the outer surface.

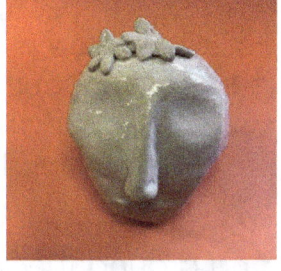
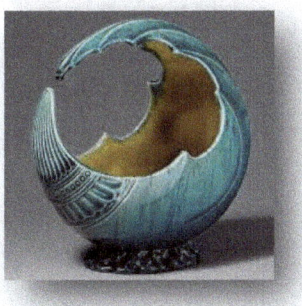
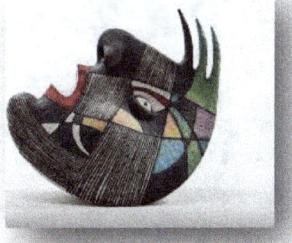
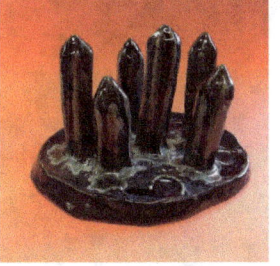
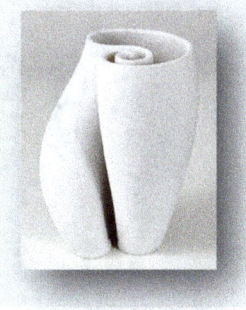

Words to Describe FORM

abstract
ambiguous
biomorphic
bulbous
cubist
cylindrical
depth
deflated
dimension
elongated
free-form
free standing
geometric
globular
inflated
interlocking
heavy
height
length
mass
nebulous
open
organic
plump
proportionate
protruding
rounded
sharp
solid
spherical
squashed
3-D
volume
width

Chapter 5 Clay Elements & Principles of Ceramic Design

SPACE

Words to Describe SPACE

atmospheric
background
closed
closer
deep
depth
dimension
farther
figure/ground
fill the frame
flat
foreground
foreshortening
further
height
horizon
illusion
length
linear perspective
mass
mid-ground
negative space
open
orthogonal
overlapping
perspective
picture plane
position
positive space
realistic
receding
shallow
size
vanishing point(s)

SPACE

The area around, above, and within an object.

ASPECTS OF SPACE

- **Positive Space** in a sculpture is the space occupied by the subject/object(s) The space which makes up the object.

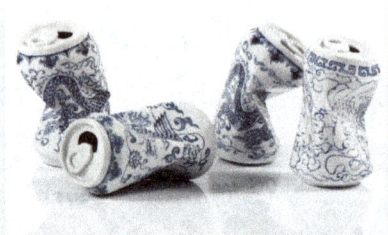

- **Negative Space** is the space in and around the solid parts of a sculpture, Negative Space can be enclosed by part of the sculpture, forming hollows or areas of emptiness, such as holes and gaps.

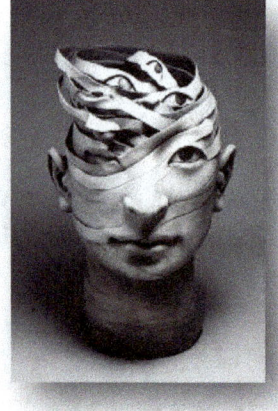
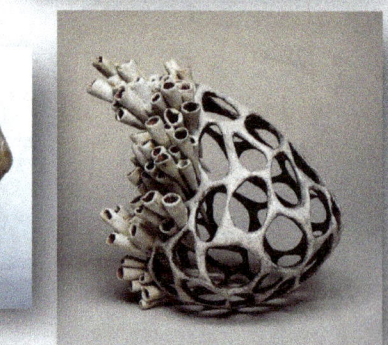

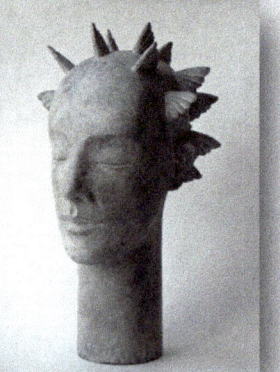
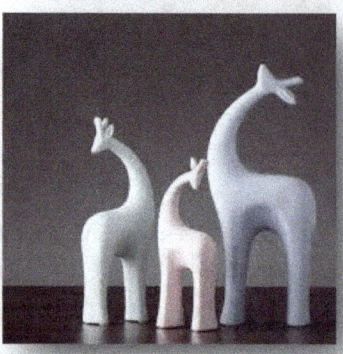

Sculptures with Multiple Pieces
Space can link separate parts of the sculpture which relate to one another across space.

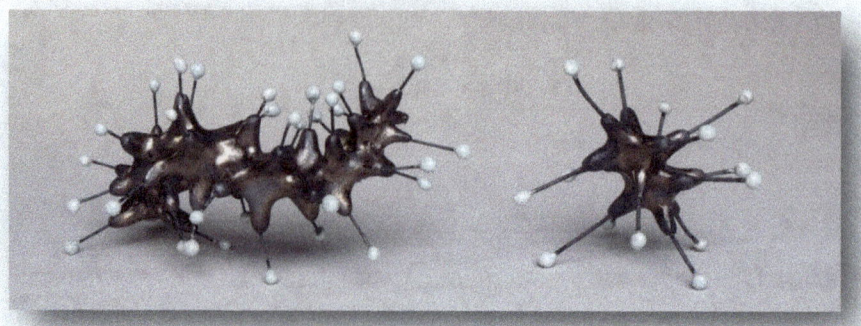

Chapter 5 Clay Elements & Principles of Ceramic Design

VOLUME & MASS

VOLUME & MASS

Three-dimensional forms have volume and mass.
Volume = a shape in three dimensions, space within that form
Mass = density of an object, actual or perceived weight

Volume

- Volume is the amount of space a form occupies. This includes both the positive and negative space of a sculpture.
- Size and shape gives a sense of volume.
- Complex sculptural forms such as a human figure and animals can have several masses or volumes that make up the form.

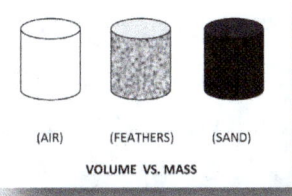
(AIR) (FEATHERS) (SAND)
VOLUME VS. MASS

Mass

- Mass is the 3D space within identifiable boundaries.
- Mass is how heavy a sculpture looks (density) together with how big it looks (volume).
- Mass can imply heaviness or lightness.
- Wide forms appear heavier than narrow forms.

Aspects of Volume and Mass

A single volume is the fundamental unit of 3D solid artworks. Some sculptures consist of only one volume, others are made of a number of volumes. The human figure is often treated by sculptors as a configuration of volumes, each of which corresponds to a major part of the body, such as the head, chest/abdomen and upper leg.

Holes and cavities in sculpture, which are as carefully shaped as the solid forms and are of equal importance to the overall design, are sometimes referred to as negative volumes.

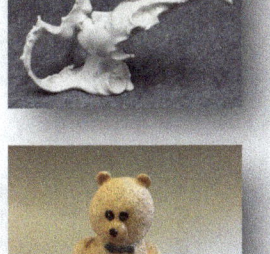
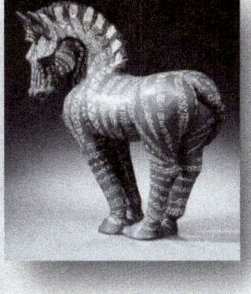
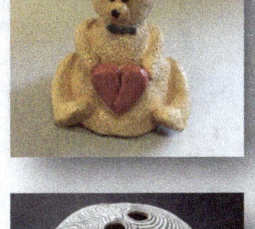
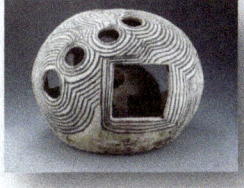
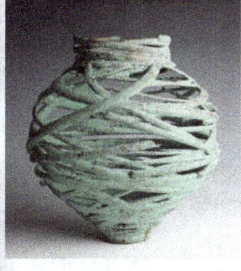
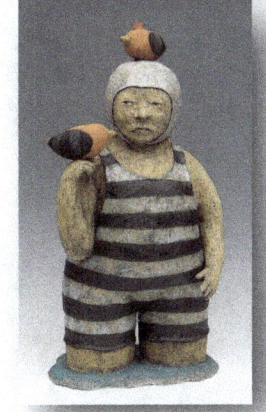
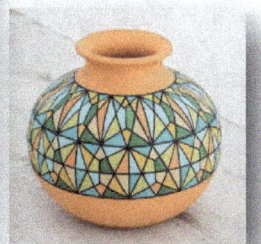

Words to Describe VOLUME & MASS

amount
block
body
bulbous
bulk
chunk
core
cubic
deflated
dimension
elongated
entirety
gob
globular
heap
inflated
heavy
height
length
lump
mass
material
open
plump
proportionate
quantity
rounded
size
spherical
solid
substance
3D
totality
volume
width

Chapter 5 Clay Elements & Principles of Ceramic Design

COLOR

Words to Describe COLOR

- analogous
- brash
- bright
- calm
- complementary
- contrasting
- cool
- dull
- dusty
- exciting
- garish
- grayed
- harsh
- hue
- intensity
- intermediate
- monochromatic
- multicolored
- muted
- neutral
- pale
- pastel
- primary
- pure
- saturated
- secondary
- shade
- subdued
- tertiary
- tinted
- triad
- value
- vibrant
- warm

COLOR
is produced when light, striking an object, is reflected back to the eye.

ASPECTS OF COLOR

Color can be used to enhance a 3D form. It can be applied as glaze, underglaze, stain, colored slip or paint or be inherent in the natural color of the clay. Color can be used to increase the clarity of the theme or meaning of a sculpture.

Colors in clay and glaze come from the minerals found in each. Glaze colors are impacted as well by the firing temperature and combination of minerals in the clay. Low-fire glazes tend to have brighter colors and higher-fire glazes more natural subtle ones.

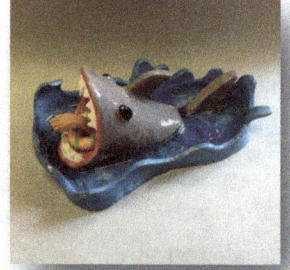
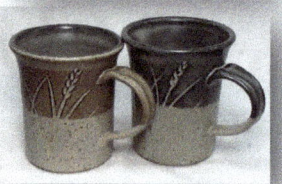
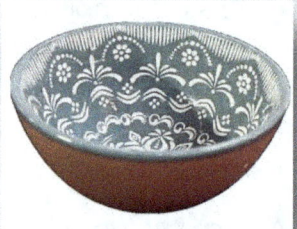

Characteristics of Color

Hue: the color itself, the distinctive quality by which one can distinguish one color from another. Examples are red, blue, green and blue.

Value: the lightness or darkness of the hue, the quality by which one distinguishes a light color from a dark one, in the range from white to black.

Chroma or Intensity: the quality that distinguishes a bold, pure hue from muted or dull one.

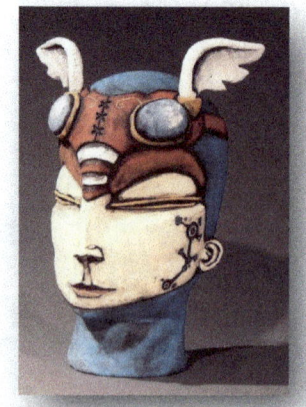
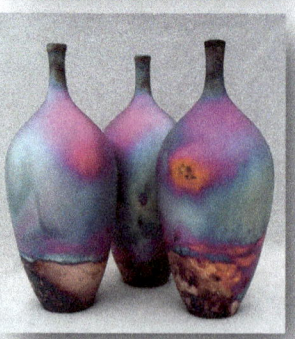
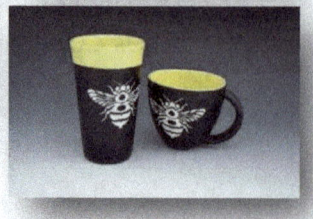

www.artboxadventures.net   artboxadventures@gmail.com

Chapter 5 Clay Elements & Principles of Ceramic Design

VALUE

VALUE

The lightness or darkness of color or an object.

ASPECTS OF VALUE

Value in art is essentially how light or dark something is on a scale of white to black (with white being the highest value and black being the lowest value).

Where do we see value in 3D Forms?

- Lightness or darkness of glaze, stain or paint on the surface of an artwork or the colors in a clay body
- Highlights or shadow on the surface of an artwork are created by the crevices of the form
- Textures and deeply carved areas have dark shadowed values; areas that stick out have light values

Types of Value

- **Subtle:** Vey little variety or contrast
- **High Contrast:** Significant differences such as black and white
- **Gradient:** Gradually changing values from light to dark or dark to light

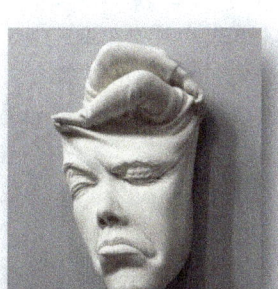
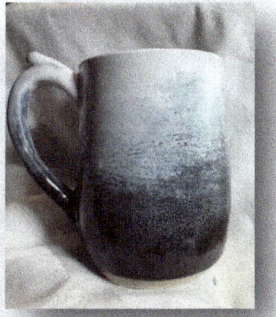
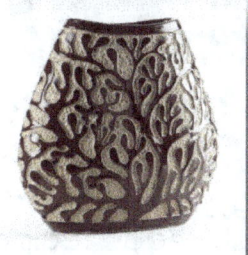
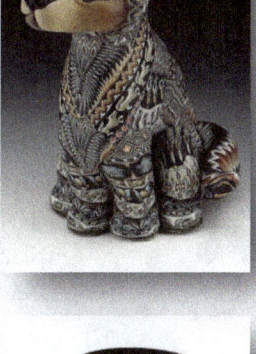
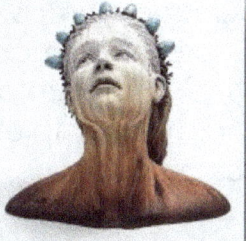
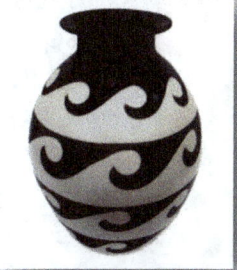
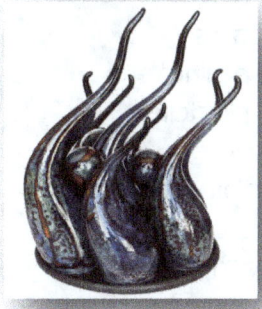
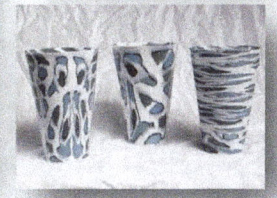

Words to Describe VALUE

bold
chiaroscuro
consistent
contrasting
crosshatching
dark
darkness
exposure
fading
faint
graduations
grey
harsh
hatching
high
Intense
light
lightness
low
luminosity
medium
opaque
range
scale
shade
shading
shadow
stippling
soft
strong
tint
tone
transparent
varied

www.artboxadventures.net — artboxadventures@gmail.com

Chapter 5 Clay Elements & Principles of Ceramic Design

TEXTURE

TEXTURE

Texture is the feel, appearance or consistency of a surface or substance. It can be actual or implied.

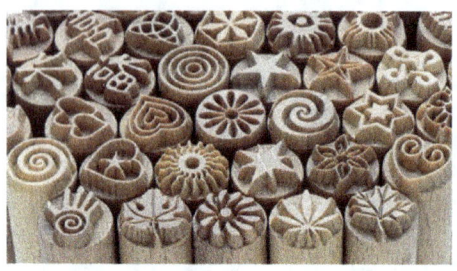

Aspects of Texture

Texture is the visual or tactile quality of a surface. We associate textures with the way things look or feel. Texture is contextual; for example smooth is smoother when contrasted with rough.

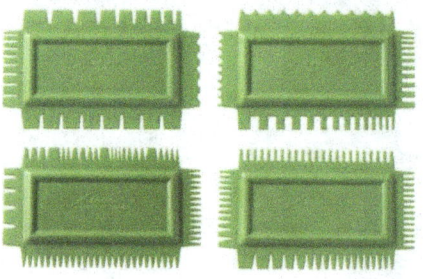

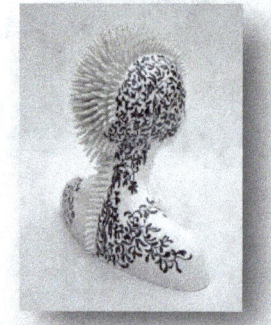 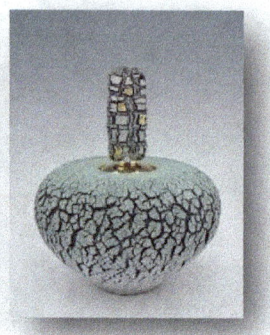

Tools to Create Texture in Clay

Textures can be created in lots of different ways. This includes using commercially made tools and stamps, but you can use items from nature or ones found around the house. Consider creating your own stamps and tools. Texture tools are often made of wood, rubber/silicone, plastic, plaster, metal or bisque-fired clay. Examples of items to create texture include:

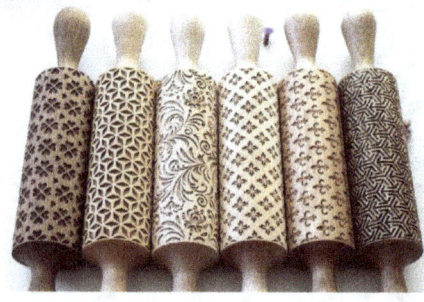

- Stamps
- Texture mats
- Texture balls
- Fluting tools
- Texture hammer
- Texture paddles
- Texture rollers
- Found objects
- Household items
- Items from nature
- Decorative ribs/combs

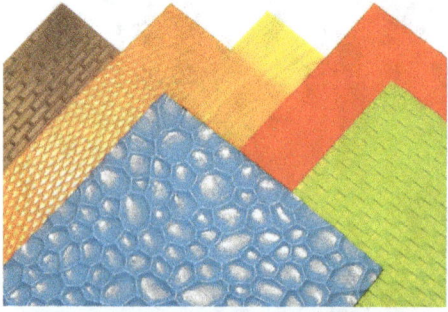

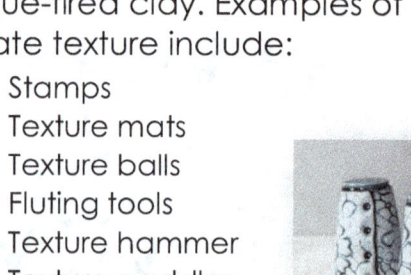

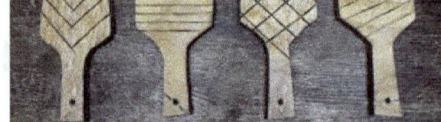

Words to Describe TEXTURE

actual
bas-relief
bristly
bumpy
dented
etched
feathery
flat
furry
gooey
gritty
hairy
implied
leathery
pitted
prickly
relief
rough
rubbing
scaly
scratchy
sgraffito
simulated
sleek
slimy
smooth
soft
stamped
sticky
tacky
tactile
toothed
velvety
woven

Chapter 5 Clay Elements & Principles of Ceramic Design

Principles of Design

The Principles of Design for Clay

are like a 'recipe' or instructions of ways to work with and organize the elements of design for functional and sculptural ceramics.

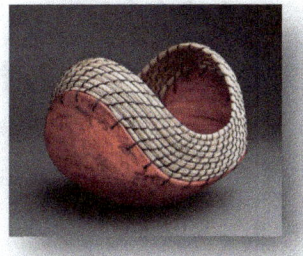

BALANCE: Ordered relationship of parts. Visual balance is achieved by the placement of similar or dissimilar parts.

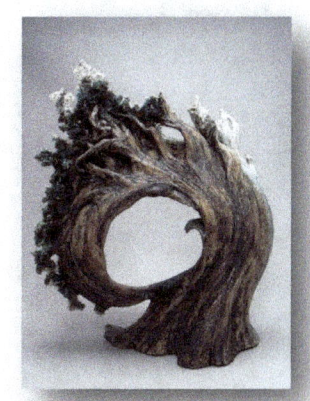

CONTRAST: Different elements used together to highlight their differences.

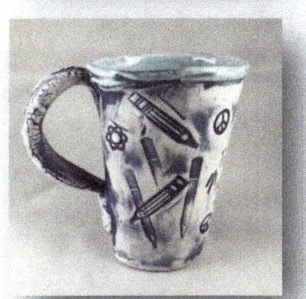

EMPHASIS: Stressing or calling attention to some part of a 3D artwork, creating a focal point.

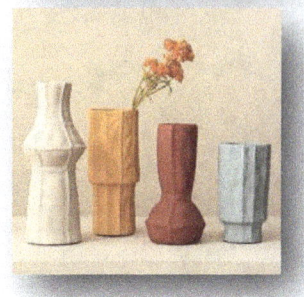

PROPORTION & SCALE: The size of the parts or whole compared one to the whole, other parts, other objects and/or the human form.

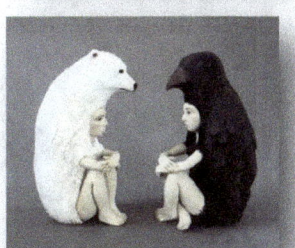

REPETITION & PATTERN: Repeating one or more elements of art to create patterns and help unify an artwork.

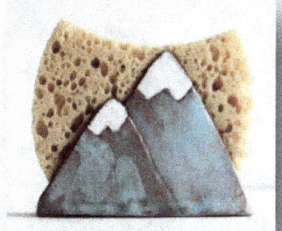

RHYTHM & MOVEMENT: Rhythm is the result of replication and creates visual interest. Movement guides the viewer's eye around the artwork.

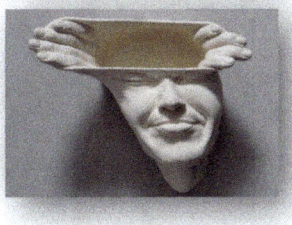

UNITY: The elements working together so everything comes together in a cohesive harmonious way.

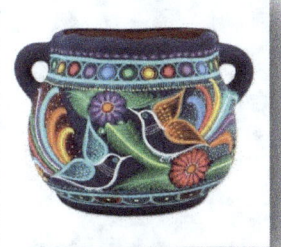

VARIETY: Using a variety of shapes, forms, textures or other elements to create visual interest.

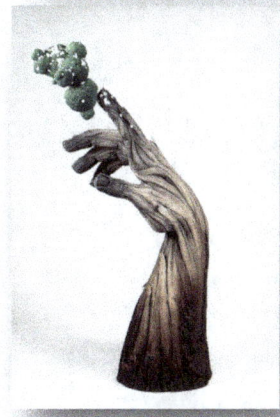

www.artboxadventures.net — artboxadventures@gmail.com

Chapter 5 Clay Elements & Principles of Ceramic Design

BALANCE

Words to Describe BALANCE

arrangement
asymmetrical
axis
bilateral
circular
cluster
distribution
equal
equality
equalization
equilibrium
evenness
formal
fulcrum
heavier
imbalance
informal
instability
lift
lighter
placement
pleasing
offset
radial
repeating
similar
stability
symmetrical
tension
uneven
visual equality
visual weight

BALANCE

Visual balance is achieved by the placement of similar or dissimilar parts.

ASPECTS OF BALANCE

Ceramic artists organize elements to distribute the visual and/or actual weight on all sides of a piece. There are three types of balance.

- **Symmetrical Balance** (equal visual units right and left/ top to bottom).

- **Asymmetrical Balance** achieved with varying size or quality of objects or parts.

- **Radial Balance** where design parts emanate from a central location.

In 3D artworks balance can be the actual weight of objects, but more commonly it is the visual weight. Examples of visual weight include:

Balance of Value: The distribution of lights and darks takes into account that dark values have stronger weight than light values

Balance of Texture: A larger area of rough texture can be balanced by a much smaller smooth area and visa versa.

Balance of Color: Warm colors tend to carry more weight than cool colors.

Balance of Shape and Form: Large shapes/forms have more weight, but several ones, even if they weigh less, can counter balance the larger shapes/forms.

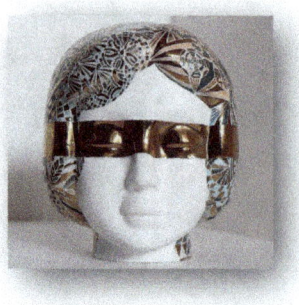
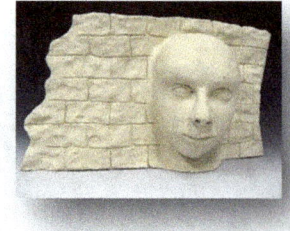
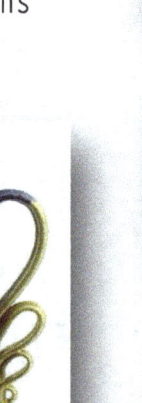
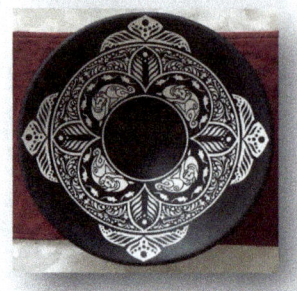
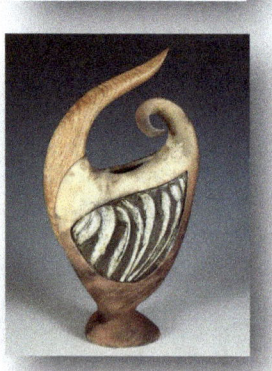
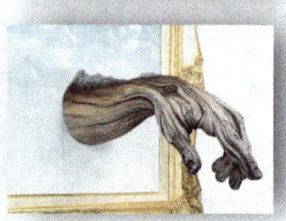
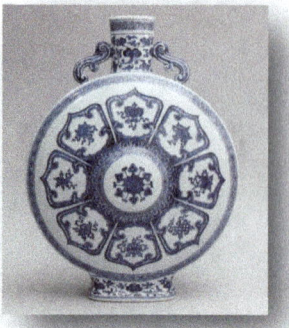

Chapter 5 Clay Elements & Principles of Ceramic Design

CONTRAST

CONTRAST

Different elements used together to highlight their differences.

ASPECTS OF CONTRAST

Contrast is one of the most dynamic of the principles of design that artists use.

Putting opposites together is a great way to draw the attention of the viewer's eye. Opposites used in ceramics include:

- light & dark values
- large & small
- wide & narrow
- complementary colors
- warm & cool colors
- bright & dull colors.

Artists often use contrast of color, shape, form, line, textures, value and direction.

Sometimes artists use high contrast for dramatic effect and other times they use medium or low contrast.

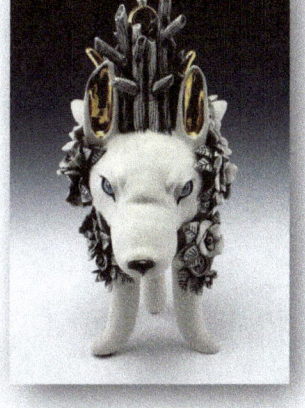
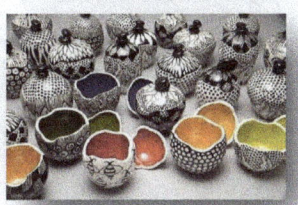
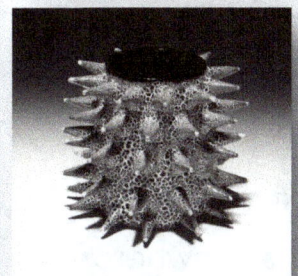
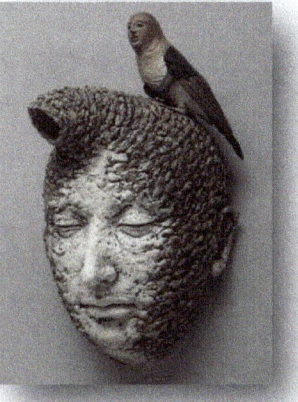
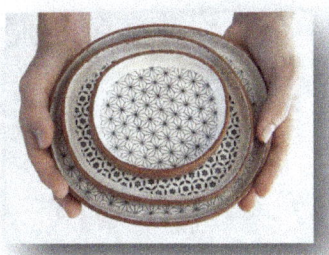
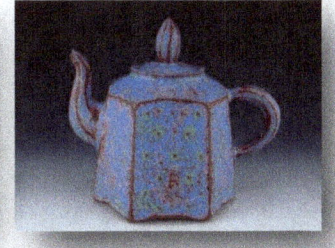

Words to Describe CONTRAST

beautiful/ugly
bold/subtle
bright/dull
centered/off-centered
detailed/simplified
difference
fine/course
geometric/organic
high/low
isolated/grouped
juxtapose
large/small
left/right
light/dark
light/heavy
long/short
many/few
near/far
opposite
organized/chaotic
rough/smooth
sharp/dull
simple/complex
stable/unstable
thick/thin
transparent/opaque
top/bottom
warm/cool
whole/broken
wide/narrow
2D/3D

www.artboxadventures.net   artboxadventures@gmail.com

Chapter 5 Clay Elements & Principles of Ceramic Design

EMPHASIS

EMPHASIS

Stressing or calling attention to some part, creating a focal point.

ASPECTS OF EMPHASIS

Emphasis is the quality that draws the viewer's attention to a certain part of an artwork. Strategically using emphasis can avoid monotony.

Ways to Create Emphasis

There are many ways to create emphasis. To make one part or area stand out consider using:

- Size, such as making one part very large

- Position, such as put something closer or in front

- Isolation, such as having one part separated from the rest of the parts

- Contrasting or bold colors

- Contrasting values

- Different or unusual textures

- A different shape than is elsewhere in the artwork

Words to Describe EMPHASIS

attention
boldness
center of interest
color
contrast
dominance
embellishment
focal point
highlighting
importance
monotony
placement
position
prominence
recede
scale
size
standout
subordinate

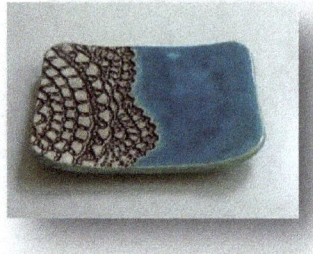
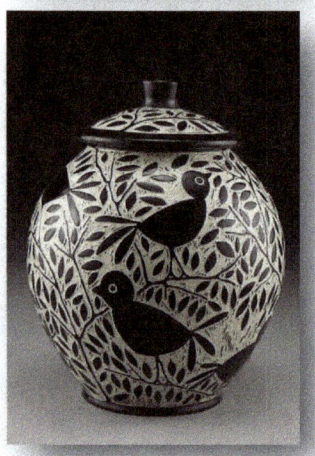
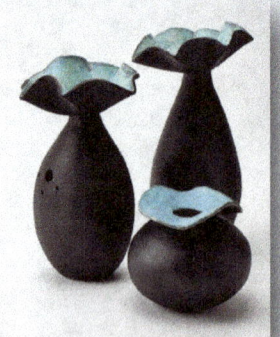
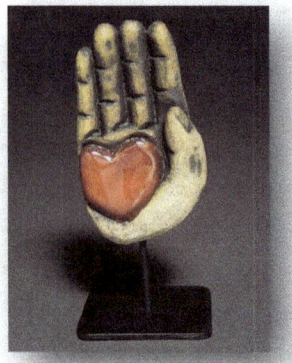
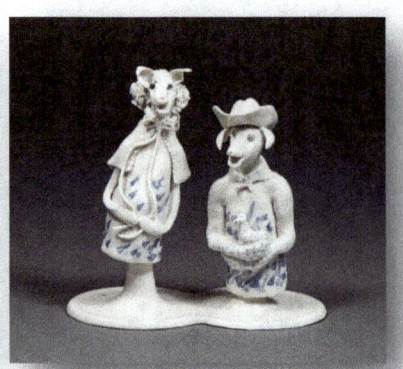
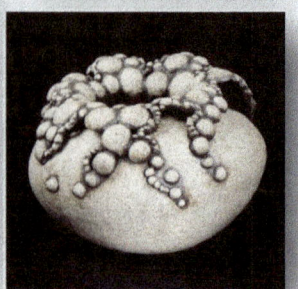
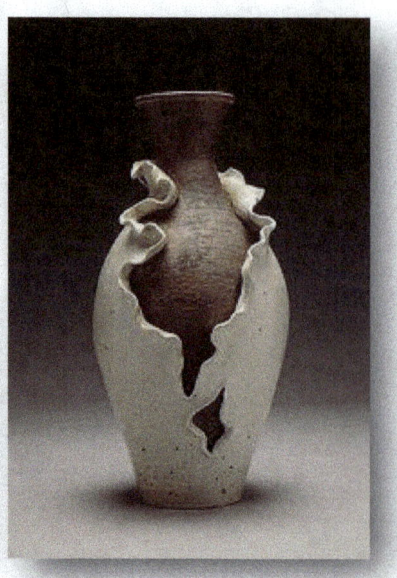

www.artboxadventures.net　　　artboxadventures@gmail.com

Chapter 5 Clay Elements & Principles of Ceramic Design

PROPORTION & SCALE

PROPORTION & SCALE

Elements compared one to another in terms of their properties of size, quantity and degree of emphasis.

Proportion is the relationship of the objects within a composition or to the whole.

Scale is the size of an object when compared to the size of a human or itself.

ASPECTS OF PROPORTION & SCALE

Proportion/Scale: Ceramic artists consider the size and relationships of the parts. Examples include the size of a head relative to its body or the size of bowl relative to what size we normally use. Artists often choose to alter proportions for dramatic effect, add visual interest, create humor or show scale.

Words to Describe PROPORTION & SCALE

amplitude
balance
comparative
dimensions
distorted
equalize
enlarge
exaggeration
foreshortening
full scale
golden ratio
grid
illusion
large scale
life size
magnitude
medium scale
miniature
minimize
monumental
parts
ratio
relationship
shrink
size
small
small scale
tall
warped
weight
whole/parts
wide

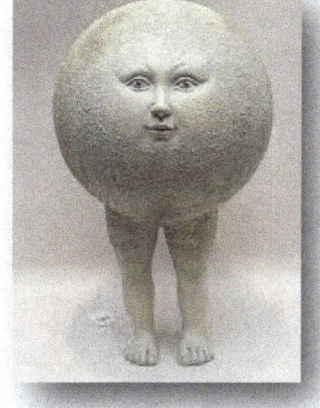
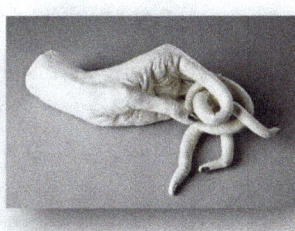
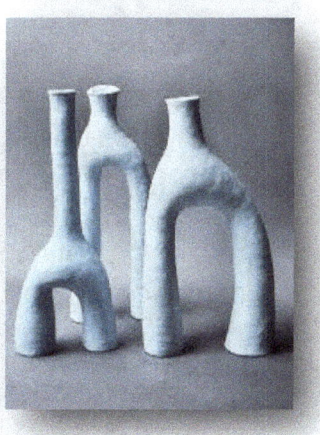
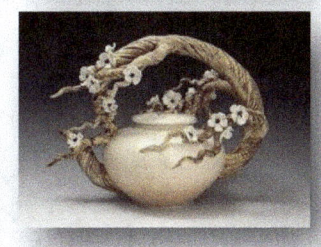
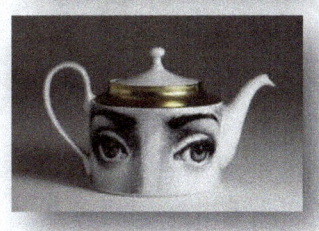
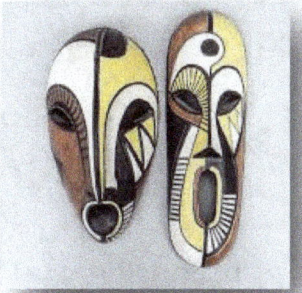

www.artboxadventures.net — artboxadventures@gmail.com

Chapter 5 Clay Elements & Principles of Ceramic Design

REPETITION & PATTERN

Words to Describe REPETITION & PATTERN

alternating
bending
consistency
curving
echo
exact
flipped
geometric
groupings
irregular
isometric
lattices
intervals
mirrored
monotonous
mosaic
motif
random
reflection
reoccurrence
repeating
rotated
slide
spacing
spirals
symmetry
tesserae
transform
translation
varied
visual beat
uniform

REPETITION & PATTERN

Repeating one or more elements of art to creates patterns and helps unify an artwork.

ASPECTS OF REPETITION & PATTERN

Repetition

Ceramic artists often use repetition of shapes, colors, lines and forms as they construct and decorate artworks.

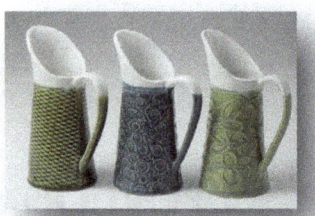

Repetition can be a great way to reinforce an idea or create a unifying effect. There is a variety of ways in which the repetition in art can occur. Repetition can be event be even or uneven, regular or irregular, it can form radiation, occurring when the repeat of elements is spread out from the central point, or a form of graduation, where the parts slowly become smaller or larger.

Pattern

Pattern is the repetition of multiple design elements working together. The elements might be reflected, rotated, flipped or translated (shifted).

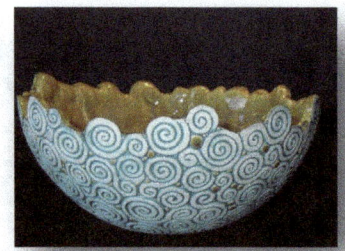

Some examples of patterns include checkered, striped, tartan, zigzag, chevron, tessellations, basketweave and herringbone. Patterns found in nature include spirals, fractals, waves, foam/bubbles, meanders and branches.

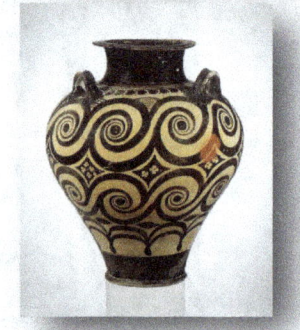
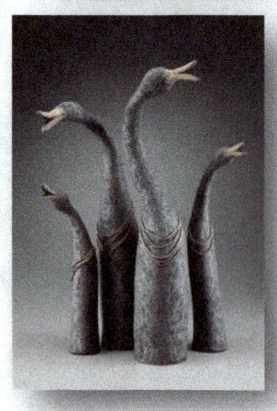

www.artboxadventures.net artboxadventures@gmail.com

RHYTHM & MOVEMENT

RHYTHM & MOVEMENT

Rhythm is created when repeating elements are used often in a deliberate pattern.

Movement is the path the viewer's eye follows in viewing an artwork.

ASPECTS OF RHYTHM & MOVEMENT

Rhythm is the visual tempo of a combination of elements when used repeatedly, and with variation. Rhythm gives the feeling of organized movement. Some rhythms create excitement and others communicate reassurance and consistency.

Types of Rhythm include:

- **Random:** Groupings of similar motifs or elements that repeat with no regularity with no discernable pattern.
- **Regular:** created by a series of elements, often identical or similar, that are placed at regular or similar intervals.
- **Alternating:** follow a set of patterns that repeat, but there is variation between the actual elements.
- **Flowing:** created by undulating elements and intervals, bending and curving motifs and spaces.
- **Progressive:** change as they go along, with each change adding to the previous iterations.

Rhythmic devices include:

- **Duplication** of the same specific element.
- **Alternately** Using 2-3 specific elements.
- **Sequential** change of a an element such changing from small to large.

Movement can be created with rhythm when using a variation of an element(s) repeatedly. Movement can also be created by strategic placement of parts to guide the viewer around the artwork. Using curved land diagonal lines or forms creates more movement compared to straight ones.

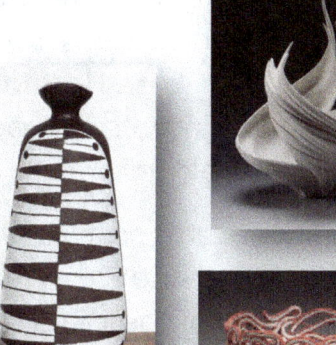
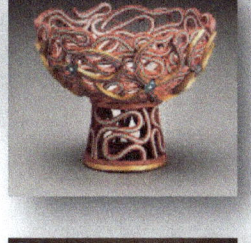
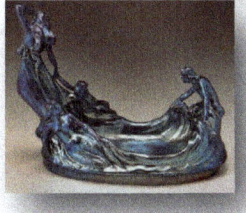
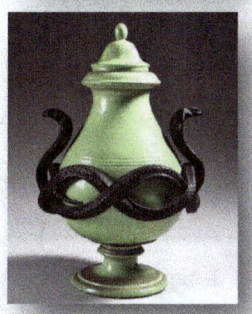
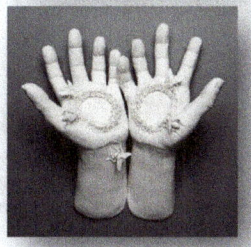

Words to Describe RHYTHM & MOVEMENT

active
around
arrangement
bending
calm
curving
directed
directional
dynamic
edges
energy
exciting
eye
flow
guide
irregular
leading
meanders
monotony
motion
mood
regular
restful
path
pattern
progressive
slow
through
transforming
transition
undulating
uniform

Chapter 5 Clay Elements & Principles of Ceramic Design

UNITY

Words to Describe UNITY

accord
alignment
chaotic
cohesion
complementary
completeness
confusion
connection
consistency
continuance
correlate
discord
disconnection
dissonant
disunity
harmony
homogeneous
integrated
interrelationship
linked
oneness
parts
peace
proximity
related
repetition
sameness
similar
sum
unified
uniform
wholeness

UNITY
The overall cohesiveness of a work of art and using the elements to create that unity.

ASPECTS OF UNITY

Unity refers to the repetition of particular elements throughout a design — whether they're colors, shapes or materials — to pull the look together. Harmony is the sense that all of the elements of a design fit and belong together.

To unify ceramic artworks, artists generally repeat an element in the structure and/or the surface of the piece.

Unity gives structure to an artwork. Ways to unify an artwork include:

- Making similar lines and shapes that repeat (curved lines with curved shapes)

- Selecting colors with a common hue (light blue, medium blue and dark blue)

- Using only one or a few values or colors

- Adding textures with similar feel and/or not using too many textures

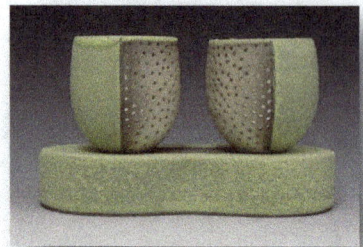
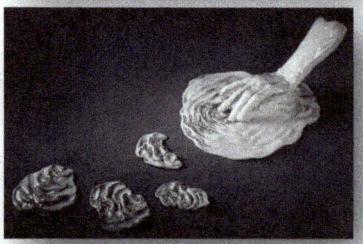
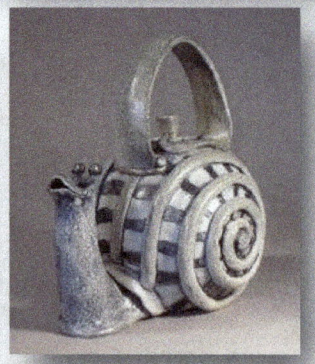
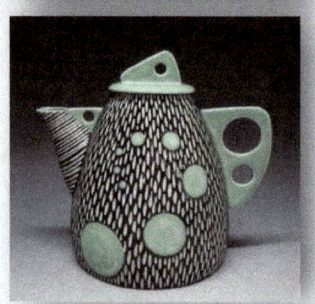
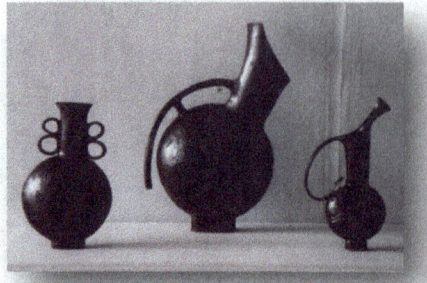
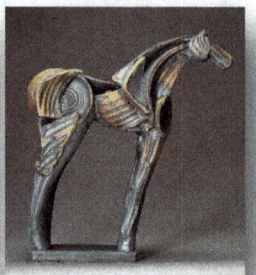
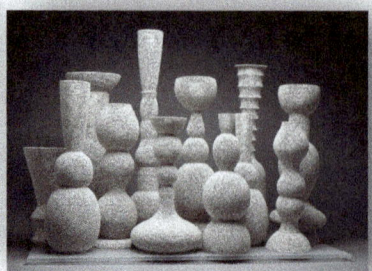

www.artboxadventures.net　　　　artboxadventures@gmail.com

Chapter 5 Clay Elements & Principles of Ceramic Design

VARIETY

VARIETY

Combining different elements to create visual interest.

ASPECTS OF VARIETY

Variety is the difference of any elements within a design.

Using a variety of shapes, forms, textures, colors or other elements helps to create visual interest. Without variety, a design can become monotonous or boring. Variety for the sake of variety is pointless and too much can make an artwork seem chaotic.

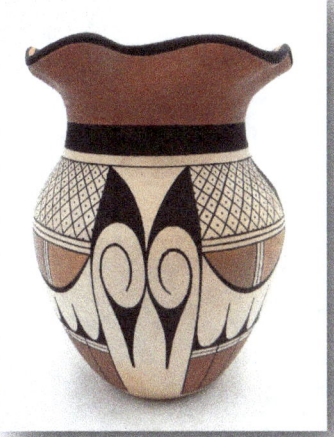

Words to Describe VARIETY

array
assortment
collection
diversity
elaboration
medley
mixture
sameness
uniformity
variation

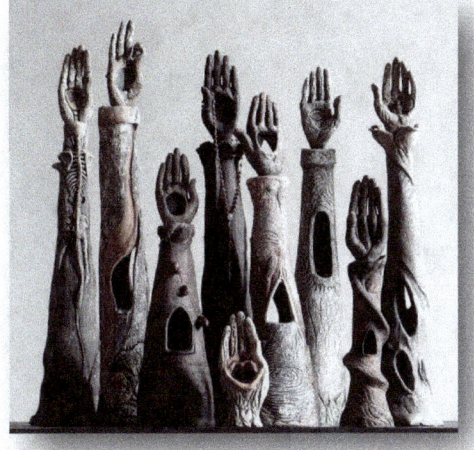

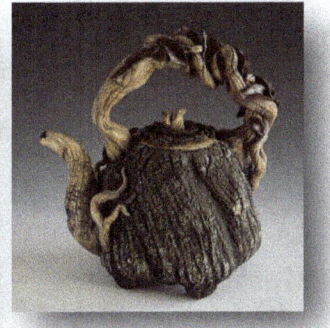

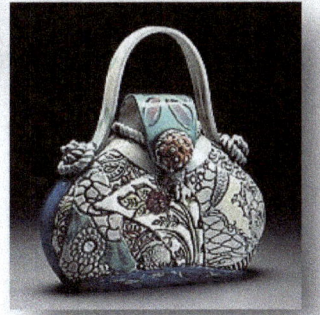

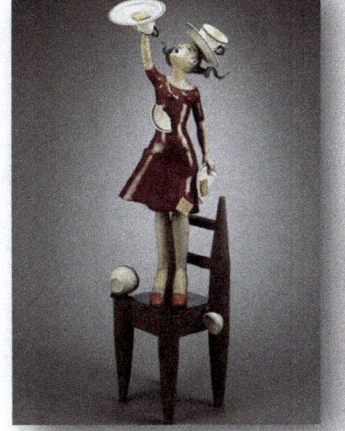

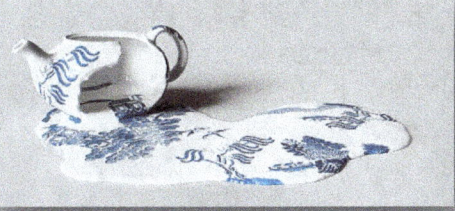

Variety and Unity

"A composition that lacks of any unifying element will nearly always seem chaotic and haphazard. A composition that is totally unified, without the relief of variety will nearly always be boring. Theses two overriding principles of design (unity and variety) are like two sides of the same coin."

Marjorie Elliot Bevlin
"Design Through Discovery"

Chapter 5 Clay Elements & Principles of Ceramic Design

Surface Design Terms

Surface Design

Artists consider multiple aspects of surface as they design and create clay artworks. They decide if the surface will be:
- Smooth or Textured
- Convex or Concave
- Flat or Curved
- Matte or Glossy
- Colorful, Muted or Left Natural.

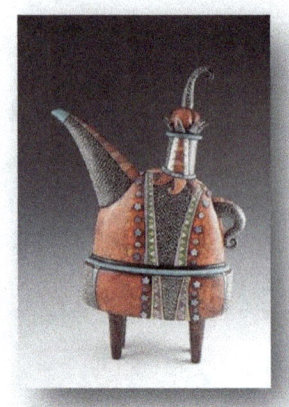

Expressive Qualities of Surfaces

Smooth vs Textured

Smooth surfaces carry no suggestion of three-dimensionality. Rough or modelled/textured surfaces show light/shadow-catching ridges or hollows.

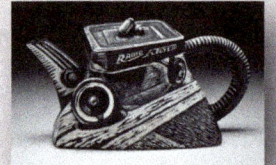

Convex vs Concave

Convex surfaces express contentment, satiety, internal pressure and general "fullness." Concave surfaces suggest external pressure, an inner insubstantiality and possible collapse.

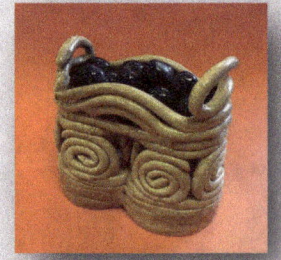

Flat vs Curved

Flat surfaces tend to be static and convey a feeling of material hardness and rigidity. They may seem unbending, unyielding and unaffected by either internal or external pressures. Curved surfaces are often more dynamic and under the influence of external forces. They are associated with growth, with expansion into space.

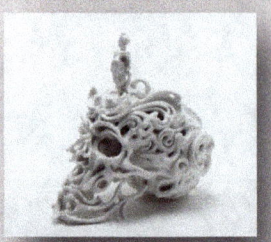

Glossy vs Matte

Glossy refers to a glaze surface that is shiny and reflects light. Matte describes a surface that has no shine and absorbs light with no reflection. The degree of shine impacts colors, and can make something look shiny and new or antiqued and old.

Color

The coloring of clay artworks may be either natural or applied. Colors of glazes vary from bright and bold to earthy and subtle. Some artists work with materials in ways that showcase their natural properties, including color and texture. Bright, artificial coloring is an important element in the design of some clay artworks. The color used on a surface can evoke emotion or clarify an idea/concept.

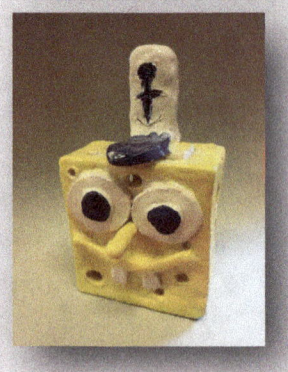

www.artboxadventures.net   artboxadventures@gmail.com

Chapter 6: Ceramic Studio Tips

Ceramics Studio Tips

15 Ideas for the Ceramics Studio or Classroom

Chapter 6: Ceramic Studio Tips

CERAMIC STUDIO TIPS

CERAMIC STUDIO HACKS

Looking for ideas to help your ceramics studio or classroom run more smoothly? Check out these 15 ideas.

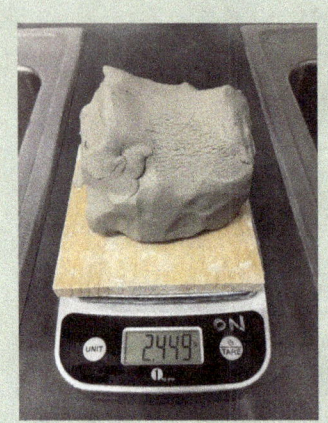

Studio Tip #1

A small scale for measuring clay is a great way to help students get a suitable amount of clay for a given artwork. For example 1.5 pounds for working on the wheel or loading the hand-held extruder. It can also be used for calculating the specific gravity of glaze.

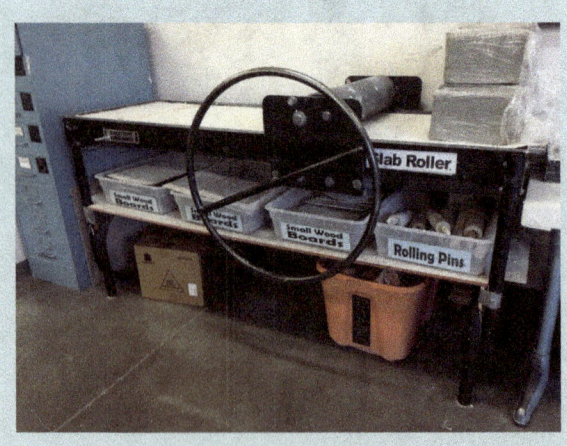

Studio Tip #2

Need extra storage? Consider adding a shelf under your slab roller to hold small clay boards, rolling pins and slats or supplies for your art studio.

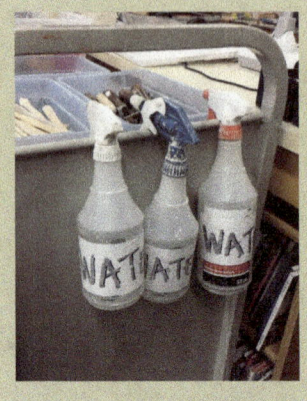

Studio Tip #3

Squirt bottles filled with water are great to moisten clay. Their handles can hook on a cart for convenient storage. (Note: This might not be suitable if you have immature students who would be tempted to squirt their friends.)

CERAMIC STUDIO TIPS

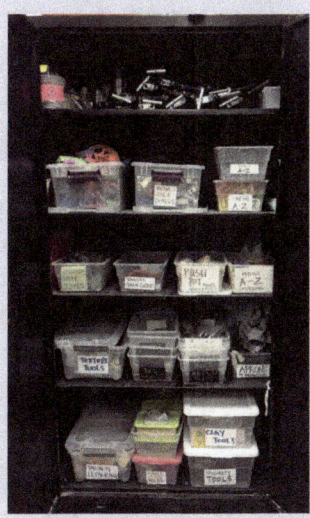

Studio Tip #4

Plastic totes are great for organizing and storing specialty tools like metal and plastic cookie cutters and different sizes of lettering stamps. This cabinet also holds the handheld extruders and glass supplies for melting into clay.

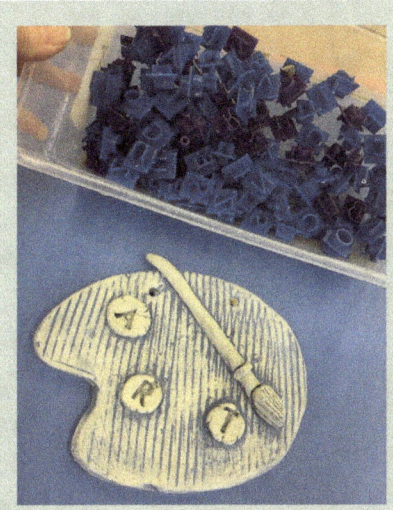

Studio Tip #5

Stepping stone lettering sets are great for doing medium sized lettering on clay artworks. Words really look professional and especially pop when stain is used on the fired surface.

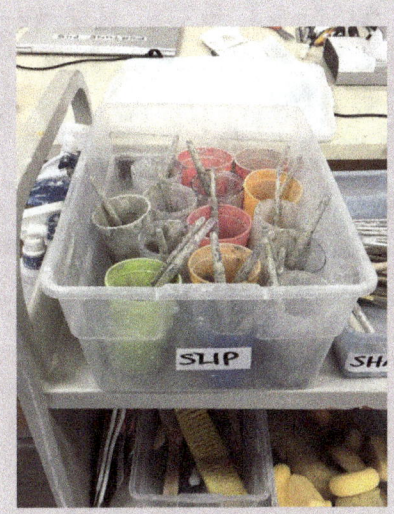

Studio Tip #6

Store slip containers in a medium sized tote box. Put the lid on the container at the end of the day. If your container is tall enough you can even keep brushes in the container. Consider purchasing durable cups from a restaurant supply store to use as slip containers.

CERAMIC STUDIO TIPS

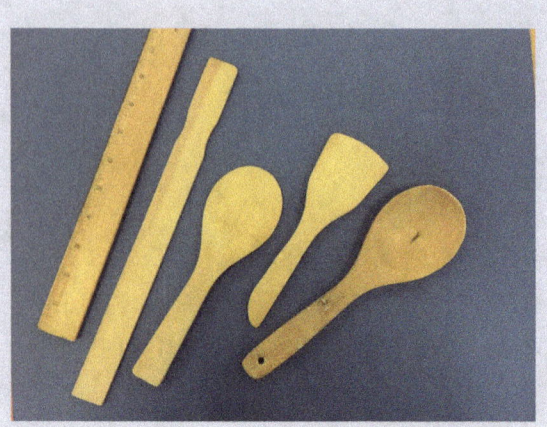

Studio Tip #7

Wooden spoons, shamoji (rice paddles), rulers and paint sticks make great paddles for altering the shape, squaring-up or removing dents of plastic or soft leather-hard artworks.

Studio Tip #8

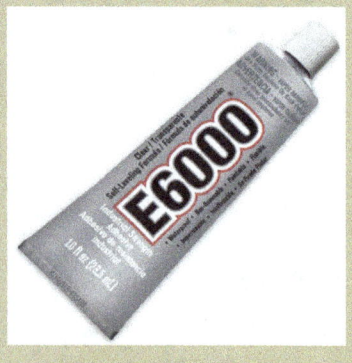
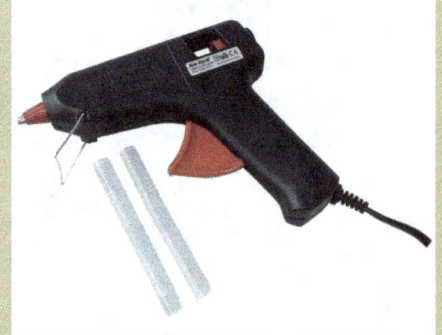

For repairing broken ceramic pieces, E6000 glue is strong and can be applied with a toothpick. It needs to dry overnight. For quicker results, hot glue can be used but it is not as strong, especially on glazed surfaces.

Studio Tip #9

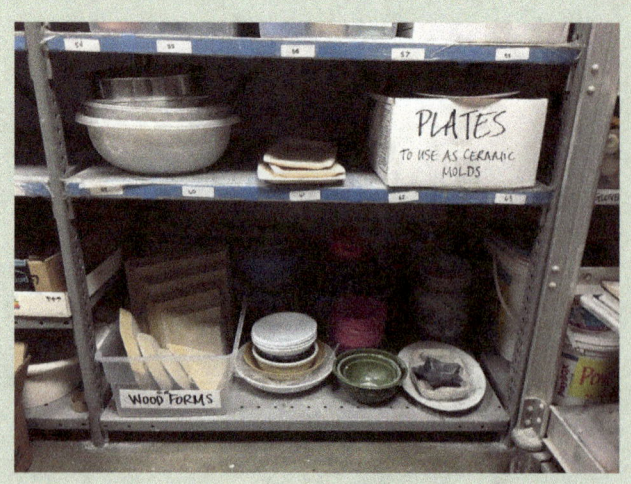

Plaster molds and wood forms are ideal for doing slump and drape molds. Start a collection of plastic, glass, metal and bisqueware bowls and plates to help create a variety of shapes and sizes. Remember to use a layer of plastic or paper towel on non-porous molds.

CERAMIC STUDIO TIPS

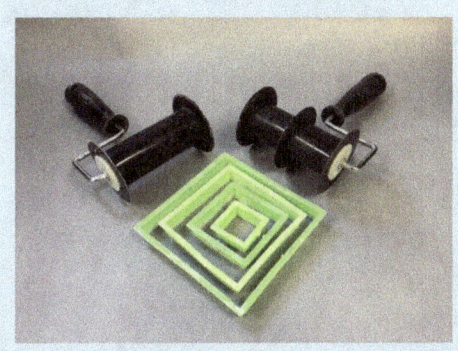

Studio Tip #10
For making tiles and small boxes, square cookie cutters and specialized 2" and 4" rollers are inexpensive options for cutting out squares.

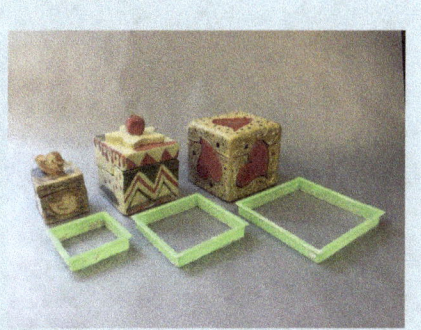

Studio Tip #11
When stamping damp clay, consider dusting the surface of the clay with corn starch. This keeps the stamp from slicking to the clay. The corn starch will burn away in the kiln.

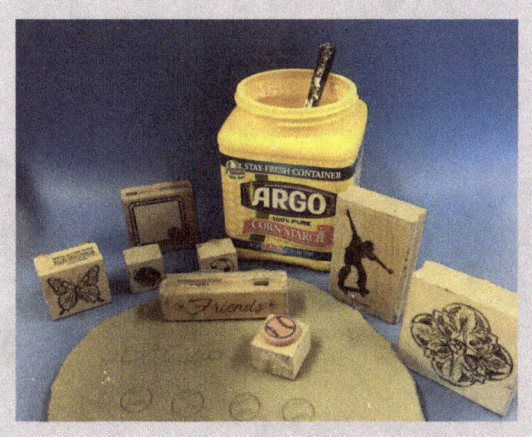

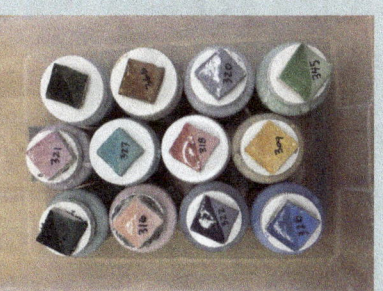

Studio Tip #12
Writing the name of the glaze in permanent marker or attaching a small test tile is an easy way for students know which glaze is in the container.

Labeling the shelves can help you know when your stock is getting low.

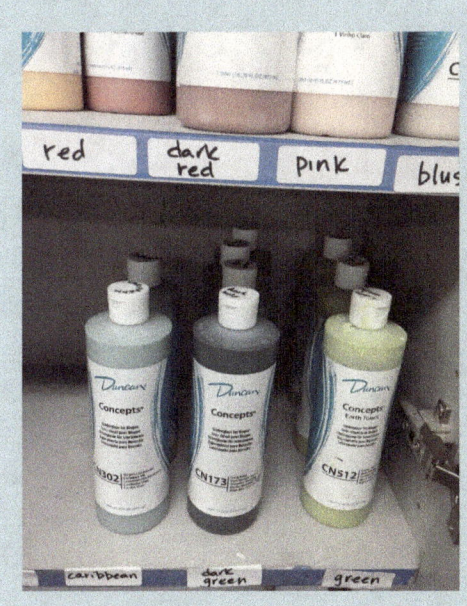

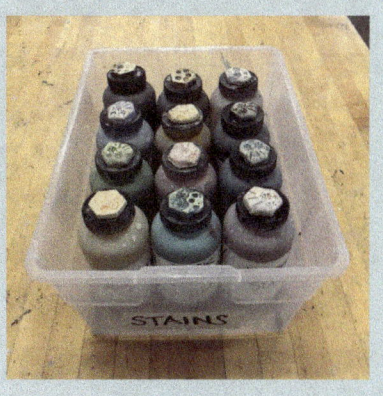

CERAMIC STUDIO TIPS

Studio Tip #13

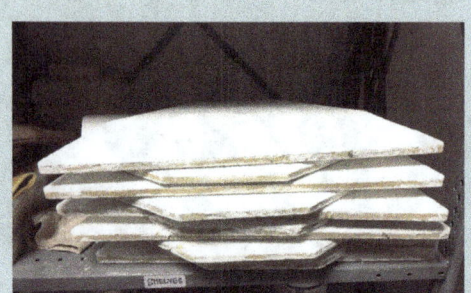
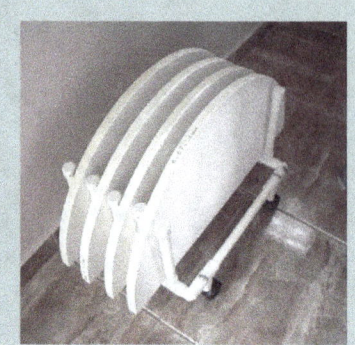

Stack your kiln shelves so they alternate direction or with a stacking system such as the PCV pipe one shown here. This makes the shelves easy to grab and you are less likely to pinch your fingers.

Studio Tip #14

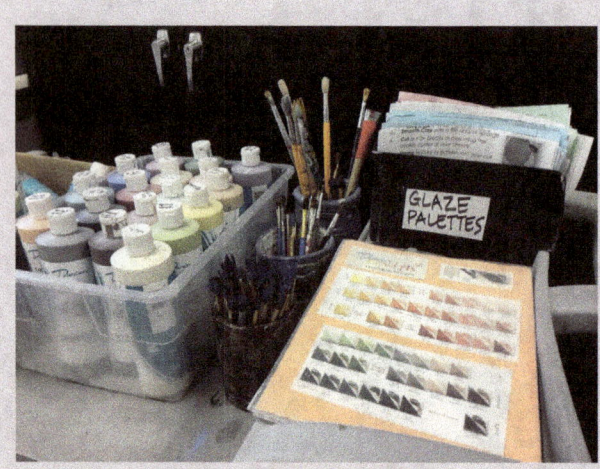

Scrap paper can make great disposable palettes if your students are using small amounts of low-fire glazes. Half sheets of 8.5 X 11 paper work well.

Studio Tip #15

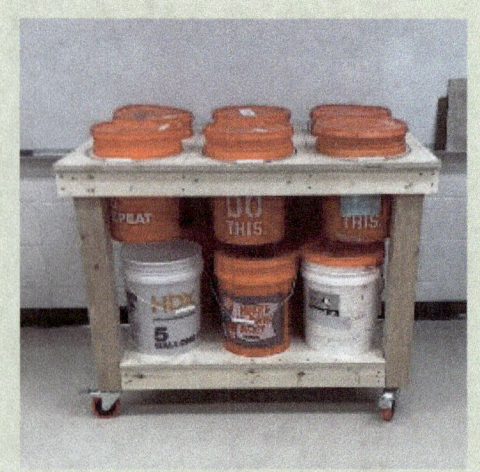

To have an organized set of 12 clay buckets, consider making a specially rolling cart. The cutout holes give the buckets on the top easy assess. The cart makes it easy to put the glazes away, especially when it is time to clear the floors.

Jim Fazio

Chapter 7: Ceramics Glossary

Glossary of Ceramic Terms

An Alphabetical Listing of Ceramic Terms and Their Meanings

7

Ceramics Glossary 1

Abstract - To simplify, emphasize or distort qualities of an actual object or figure.

Alumina - Aluminum oxide (Al_2O_3) makes up 15% of the earth's surface. When combined with silica and chemical water, it forms clay.

Antiquing - A method of applying color and wiping it back to accentuate the detailed surface.

Annealing - The process of cooling a heated object gradually to allow internal shrinkage stress to equalize without damage.

Axis - A line, real or imagined, around which the material that composes an object appears to be organized.

Bagwall - The wall deflects the flame from the ware inside a fuel-burning kiln.

Bat - A flat disc made out of plaster, wood, or plastic which is affixed to the wheel head with clay or pins.

Batch - A mixture of weighed materials such as a batch of glaze, slip or a clay body.

Banding Wheel - A revolving wheel-head which sits on a pedestal base. It is turned by hand and used for finishing or decorating pottery.

Bisque - Pottery which has been fired once, without glaze, to a temperature just before vitrification.

Bisque Fire - First firing, without glaze. Slips can be used in a bisque firing.

Bone China - A thin and translucent china, historically made from bone ash, china clay and Cornish stone.

Bone Dry - Completely air dried.

Breaking Glaze - A decorative effect in ceramic glazes that exploits changes in color and character in certain glazes when their thickness varies.

Burnishing - Polishing leather-hard clay by rubbing with a smooth stone or back of a spoon, etc.

Calipers - A tool used to measure the diameter of round forms. For example, calipers are used to get lids to fit just right.

Casting - A clay form made from a mold. May also refer to plaster castings.

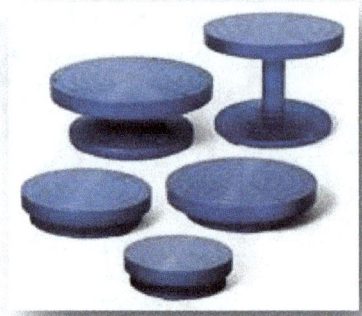
Banding Wheel

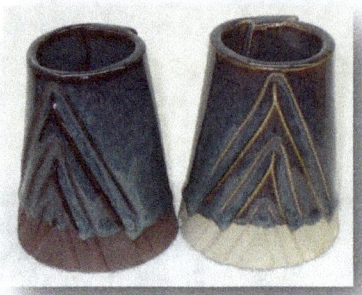
Breaking Glaze

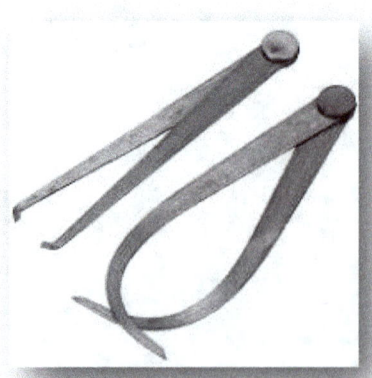
Calipers

Ceramics Glossary 2

Centering - Technique to move the clay so it is symmetrically rotating in the middle of a wheel head so you can then make a cylinder or other pottery.

Ceramics - Items made from a non-metallic mineral and fired at a high temperature.

Chuck - A chuck is a form that can hold a pot upside-down above the wheel head while the potter trims it. Chucks are bisque-fired clay cylinders which are open on both ends.

Ceramics - Clay forms that have been fired in a kiln.

China - A term that usually refers to the bone china of England, but also is associated with vitreous white wares and porcelain.

Clay - Material made of Alumina + Silica + Water that when heated at a high temperature becomes ceramics.

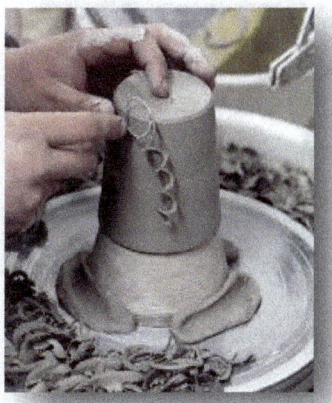

Breaking Glaze

Clay Body - A mixture of different types of clays and minerals for a specific ceramic purpose. For example, porcelain is a translucent white clay body.

Clay Dust - A very fine dust that can linger in the air for days. Prolonged exposure to clay dust can cause silicosis or lung disease. Prevent clay dust from accumulating in the studio, we clean up clay using water, a wet mop or wet sponge. Never sweep in the clay studio!

Coil - A piece of clay rolled like a rope, used in making pottery.

Compress - Pushing the clay down and together, forcing the particles of clay closer.

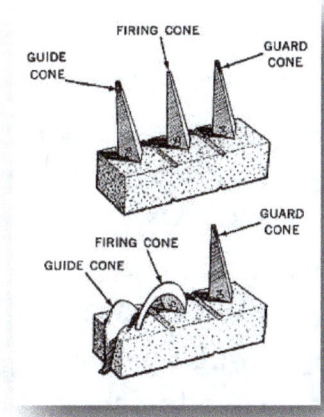

Cones

Composite Pots - Pots that were thrown or hand-built in separate pieces and then assembled.

Cone - A small pyramid composed of clay and glaze, made to melt and bend at specific temperatures. It is used in a kiln to determine the end of a firing. In some electric kilns, it shuts off a kiln setter.

Coning - Squeezing the clay upward into a cone-like shape when working on the wheel.

Contour - The outline of an object.

Craftsmanship - Skill, attention to detail and quality workmanship in use of tools and materials.

Craters - Bubbles on the surface of glaze finish that have popped.

Crazing - The cracking of a glaze on a fired pot. It is the result of

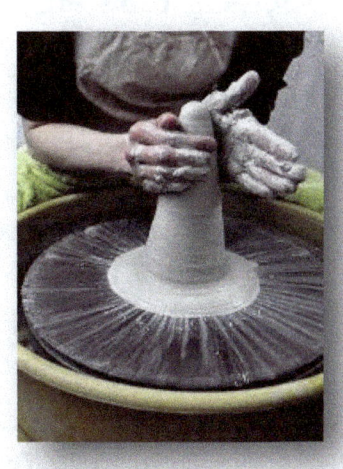

Coning

Ceramics Glossary 3

the glaze shrinking more than the clay body in the cooling process.

Crawling - A bare spot (on a finished piece where oil or grease prevents the glaze from adhering to pottery.

Damper - A slab of refractory clay used to close or partially close the flue of a kiln.

De-Airing - The process of removing air from plastic clay using a pugmill. It makes the clay denser and more plastic.

Dry Brushing - Applying glaze or underglaze with a dry brush to produce a feather-like effect.

Dry Foot - Keep bottom of a pot free from glaze by waxing or removing the glaze.

Earthenware - A low-fire clay, that absorbs water and is normally fired below 2,190 °F (1200 °C). When red in color it is called terracotta. Also available in white.

Element - The heating coils of an electric kiln.

Engobe - Colored clay slip used to decorate greenware or leather-hard pieces before bisque-firing. It is made of clay, oxide and water.

Extrude - Shaping clay or other pliable material by forcing it through a die.

Extruder - Barrel-shaped equipment used to make coils of assorted shapes and sizes as well as hollow forms.

Faceting - Cutting away broad strips of clay using a knife, faceting tool or wire-cutter on the outer surface of a pot.

Faceting Tools - Tools designed to cut away broad strips of clay.

Fettling Knife – A tool used for trimming rough edges of pottery before firing which is also handy for cutting and texture making.

Fire - To heat a clay object in a kiln to a specific temperature.

Firebrick - An insulation brick used to hold the heat in the kiln and withstand high temperatures.

Firing - The process by which ceramic ware is heated in a kiln to bring glaze or clay to maturity.

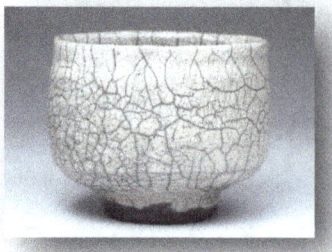
Crazing

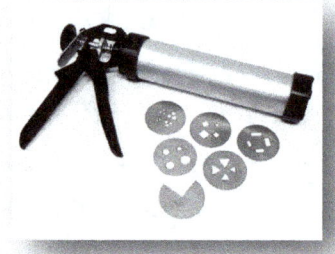
Extruder

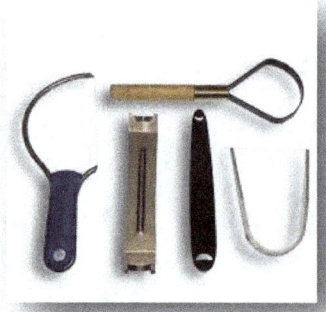
Faceting Tools

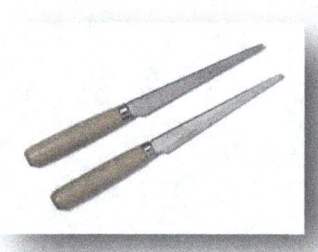
Fettling Knife

Chapter 7: Ceramics Glossary

Ceramics Glossary 4

Firing Range - The temperature at which a clay body becomes mature or a glaze melts.

Flux - A melting agent causing silica to change into a glaze. It is used to lower the melting point of glazes.

Food-safe - A product that has been tested and determined to be safe for use on surfaces that come in contact with food or drink.

Foot - Base of a ceramic form.

Frit - A glaze material derived from flux and silica that is melted together and reground into a fine powder. Frit added to a body or a glaze lowers its melting point.

Glaze - A thin coating of glass. An impervious silicate coating, which is developed by the fusion under heat of inorganic materials.

Glaze Firing - The final firing, with glaze.

Gloss Glaze - A shiny reflective gloss.

Geometric - Mechanical, human-made shapes with regular edges such as squares, circles, triangle and polygons.

Greenware - Unfired pottery. Ready to be bisque-fired.

Grog - A sand-like granular material that is made from fired clays, added to clay to reduce shrinkage and gives clay added strength and texture.

Hot Spot - A section of a kiln that fires to a hotter temperature than the rest of the kiln.

Incise - Decorations carved into the surface of clay creating low relief.

Juxtaposition - Placement side by side; relationship of two or more elements in a composition.

Kalolin - The purest of natural clays. Also known as China Clay. Used in porcelain clay bodies.

Key - Pair of concave and convex bumps that interlock.

Kinetic - Construction that contains moving elements set in motion by air, motors or gravity.

Kiln - A furnace of refractory clay bricks for firing pottery and for fusing glass.

Kiln Furniture - Posts, stands and shelves used for stacking pottery in the kiln for firing.

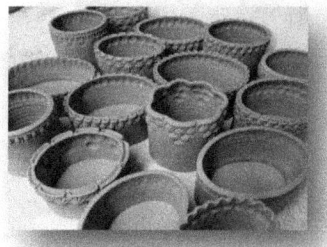
Greenware

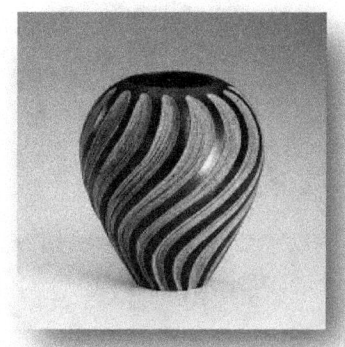
Incise

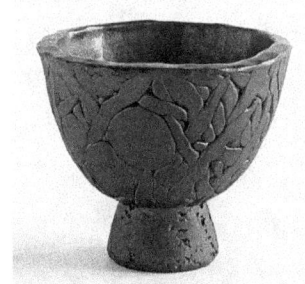
Footed Bowl

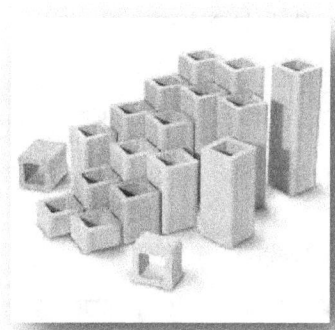
Kiln Posts

Ceramics Glossary 5

Kiln Shelves - Shelves inside the kiln which are coated with kiln wash to keep glazed projects from sticking.

Kiln Sitter (automatic shut-off) - A device used with a pyrometric cone to shut off the kiln when conditions inside the kiln cause the cone to bend.

Kiln Wash - Mixture of kaolin, flint and water. It is painted on one side of the kiln shelves to separate glaze drips from the shelf.

Leather-Hard - Stage of the clay between plastic and bone dry. Clay is still damp enough to join it to other pieces using slip. For example, this is the stage handles are applied to mugs.

Majolica - A low-fire glazing technique. The process involves applying an opaque tin glaze to earthenware and painting it with different colored oxides.

Malleable/Malleability - The capability of being molded, taking shape or being made to receive desired form.

Maquette - A small, scale model for a work intended to be enlarged.

Maturing Point - The temperature at which the clay becomes hard and durable.

Mishima - Inlaid clay achieved by carving, applying a different colored slip and then sanding the surface.

Matte - A glaze surface that is dull/soft, reflecting little shine. The opposite of glossy.

Matte Glaze - A dull glaze surface, not very reflective when fired. It needs a slow cooling period or it may turn shiny.

Mold - A plaster shape designed to pour slip cast into and let dry so the shape comes out as an exact replica of the mold.

Nesting - The procedure of stacking greenware in a kiln during the bisque-firing.

Opaque Glaze - A glaze you can not see through to the surface, color or texture beneath.

Opacity - How transparent or opaque a glaze is. Knowing this will help you get the effect you want for the surface of your piece.

Opaque - Non-transparent.

Organic - Free forms representing living things that have irregular edges. Also, biomorphic.

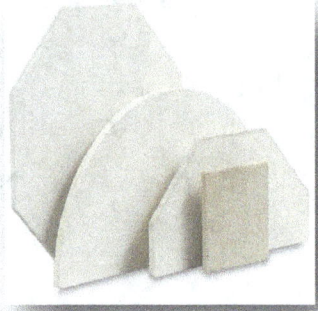
Kiln Shelves

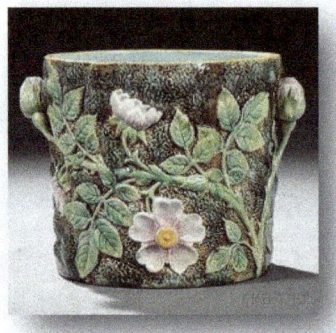
Majolica

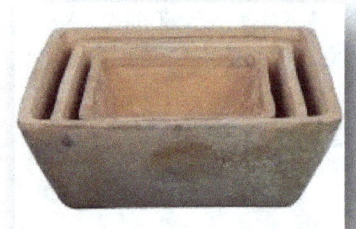
Nesting

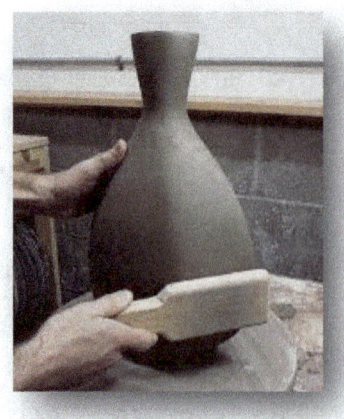
Paddling

Ceramics Glossary 6

Oxidation - Firing with a full supply of oxygen. Electric kilns fire in oxidation.

Oxides - Metal oxides can be mixed with water and applied to clay. They are often used to stain the clay, by applying it on and then wiping most of it off.

Paddling - Shaping a soft or medium leather-hard piece by gently hitting with a wooden paddle to achieve the form you want. Sometimes the paddle is textured to create flat facets or to resolve irregularities in the surface.

Peephole - A small observation hole in the wall or door of a kiln.

Pierced or Perforated - Clay with cut out holes, usually done with a sharp tool or cookie cutter.

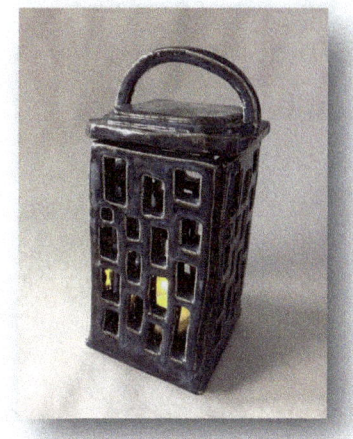
Pierced

Pinch - Manipulating a clay by pinching with your fingers in your palm to create a hollow form.

Pinch Pot - A technique used to create small bowl-like shapes using a pinching motion.

Pin Holes - Tiny holes in the final surface finish of a glaze or underglaze.

Plasticity - The quality of clay which allows it to be manipulated into different shapes without cracking or breaking.

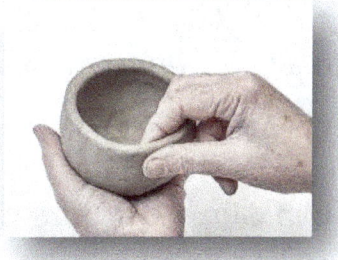
Pinch Pot

Platelets - The microscopic particles that make up clay. The size and shape of the particles determines the plasticity of the clay.

Porcelain - White stoneware, made from clay prepared from feldspar, china clay, flint and whiting.

Pot Lifters - A pair of angular metal tools used to help remove a pot from the potter's wheel when finished throwing it.

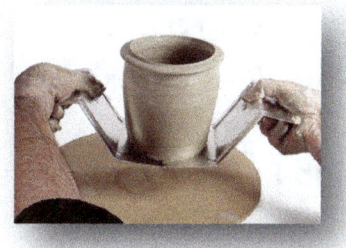
Pot Lifters

Potter's (Pottery) Wheel - A device with either a manual (foot-powered) or electric rotating wheelhead used to make pottery forms.

Pug/Pugging - To mix. The mixing, blending, de-airing and extrusion of plastic clay bodies.

Pug Mill - A machine for mixing and recycling clay.

Pyrometer - A thermometer to measure heat in the kiln.

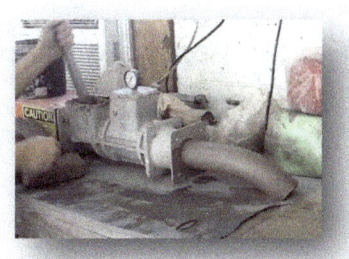
Pugging

Ceramics Glossary 7

Pyrometric Cone - Three-sided pyramid that are the kiln.

Radial - Compositions that have the major images or design parts emanating from a central location.

Raku - A type of pottery originating in Japan in the 1500s. The clay is bisque-fired and removed while red hot and glaze is molten. It is then placed in a bed of combustible materials and covered. The intense reduction results in irregular surfaces and colors.

Reduction - Firing with reduced oxygen in the kiln.

Refractory Material - Substances that have a resistance to high temperatures.

Rib - A rubber, metal or wooden tool used to facilitate wheel throwing of pottery forms or smoothing clay.

Relief - When forms project from or are carved into a surface.

Relief Sculpture - Sculptures that have forms projecting from a background that are usually mounted on a wall.

Satin Glaze - A glaze with medium reflectance, between matte and gloss.

Scale - The relationship between the size of an object and the size of its surroundings.

Sgraffito – From the Italian word meaning 'scratched through.' Incising a design in colored slip revealing the clay body.

Slab - Pressed or rolled flat sections of clay used in hand building.

Slab Roller - Large press-like equipment used to roll even, flat pieces of clay.

Slip - Clay mixed with water to the consistency of mayonnaise. Used in casting, decoration and joining clay pieces together.

Slip Casting - Forming ceramic ware by pouring slip into molds which are typically made of plaster. Slip casting is used commonly used for mass producing a product.

Slip Trailing - A technique of adding a relief pattern to a clay surface by trailing lines of slip (clay in thick paste form) using a tube or nozzle (like cake decorating). The raised lines and strokes are often colored and create a surface that is both visually appealing and tactile.

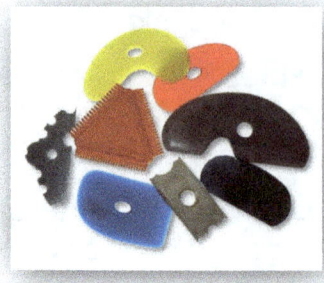
Ribs

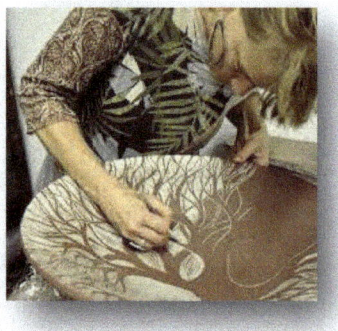
Sgraffito

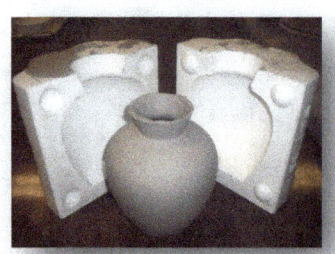
Slip Casting

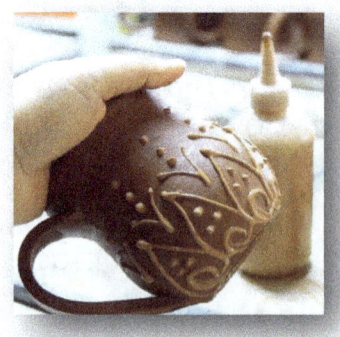
Slip Trailing

Ceramics Glossary 8

Slurry - A thick slip.

Slurry Bucket - A bucket where used clay is deposited for recycling.

Soaking - Maintaining a low, steady heat in the early stages of firing to achieve a uniform temperature throughout the kiln.

Specific Gravity - Measures how dense a substance/liquid is compared to water. Water has a specific gravity 1. To determine the specific gravity of a liquid, measure out 100 mL of the liquid and then weigh the liquid in grams. Divide this number by 100. If 100mL of slip weighs 180g, 1.8 is its specific gravity.

Stacking - Loading a kiln to hold the maximum number of pieces.

Stain - A mixture of oxide and water used as a colorant for bisqueware.

Stilt - A type of kiln furniture, which is usually triangular. When placed under a ceramic piece, it helps prevent glaze from melting on to the shelves during firing.

Stoneware - Artworks with a stone-like quality made with mid-fire or high fire clay.

Symbol - Something used for or regarded as representing something else, as in signs, emblems or tokens.

Tactile - Perceptible to touch; that which is tangible.

Terracotta - Orangish-brown earthenware clay often used for flower pots.

Texture - The tactile quality of a surface. Rough textures are often carved or stamped into clay.

Thermal Shock - Cracks in a ceramic body caused by sudden heating or cooling.

Transparent Glaze - A glaze you can see through to the surface, texture or color underneath.

Throwing - Creating ceramic shapes on the potter's wheel.

Under-Firing - Not firing hot enough or long enough, or both.

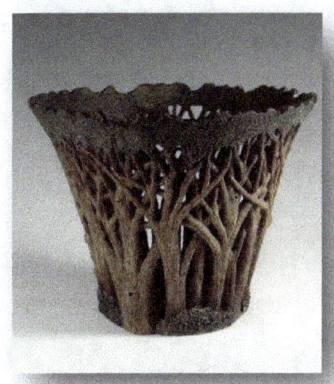

Stain

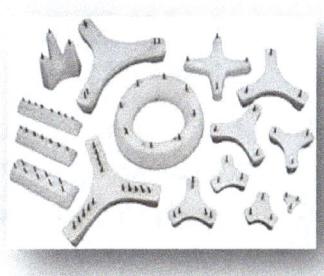

Stilts

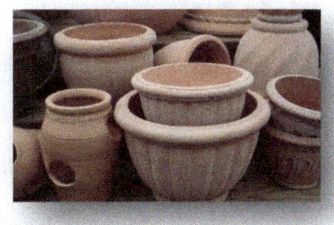

Terracotta

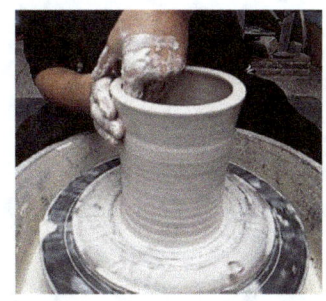

Throwing

Ceramics Glossary 9

Underglaze - Liquid clay slip that contains coloring oxides and chemicals used to apply color and designs to ceramic piece at the greenware or bisqueware stage.

Vessel - A hollow container, especially one used to hold liquids.

Viscosity - The property of a liquid to resist movement. Syrup has a high viscosity and water has a low viscosity.

Vitreous - Clay that has been fired or burnished so that it is Impervious (waterproof). It has become a "glassy" like material / body that has extremely low or no porosity.

Vitrification - The progressive fusion of clay during the firing process, turning it into hard, non-crystalline glass. As vitrification proceeds, the glassy bond increases and the porosity of the fired product becomes lower.

Void - A hollow concavity, or unoccupied space within a solid object or mass.

Wax Resist - Liquid wax that is painted onto the clay surface or onto the glaze so that anything on top of it is "resisted" or won't stick. Wax is used to create a dry foot on the bottom of a piece, or to protect an area of glaze so you can layer over it and create patterns.

Ware - A general term for pottery.

Warping - Deformation of ceramic items caused by uneven drying or overfiring.

Water Soaking - Beginning stage of the firing cycle. As pottery is heated, the last of the water is driven off.

Wedging - A method of kneading clay that uses pressure to make it homogenous, eliminates air bubbles and aligns the particles.

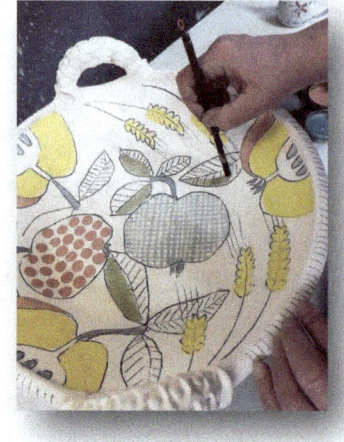
Underglaze

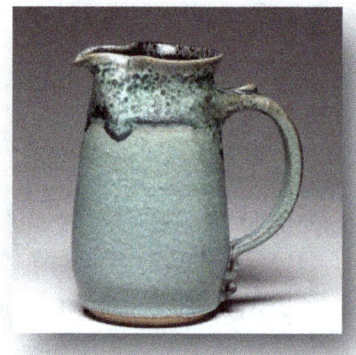
Vessel

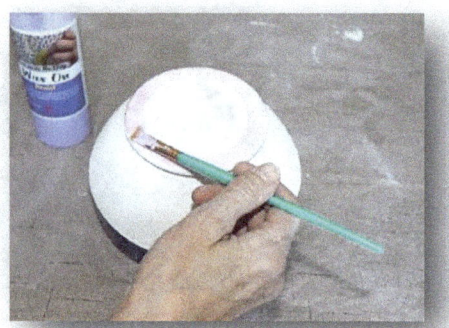
Wax Resist

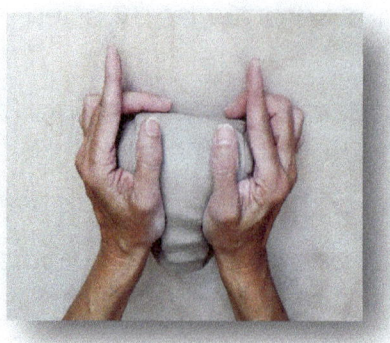
Wedging

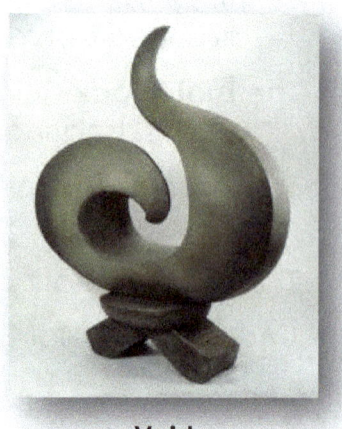
Void

"All About Clay"
Resources for Ceramics Teachers and Students

Books, PowerPoints and Posters

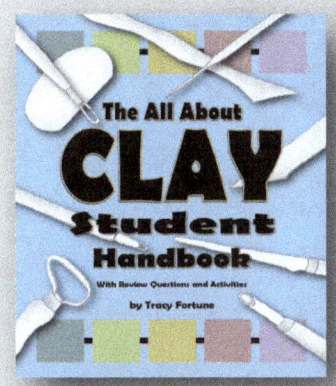 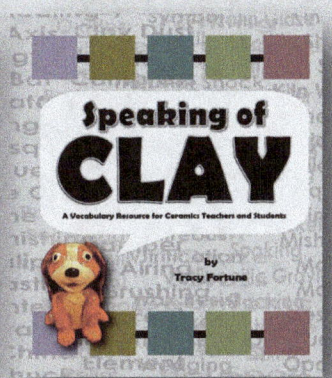 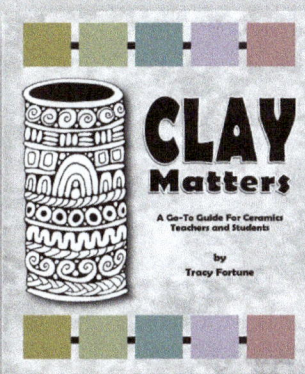 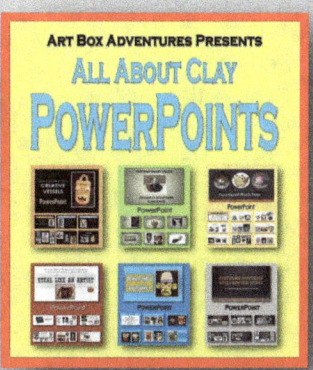

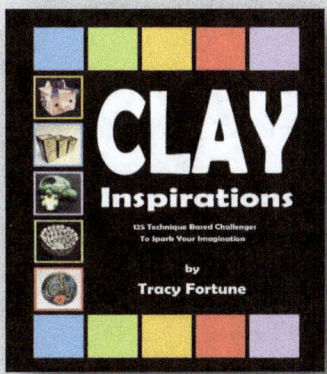 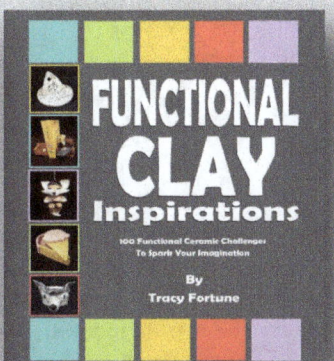 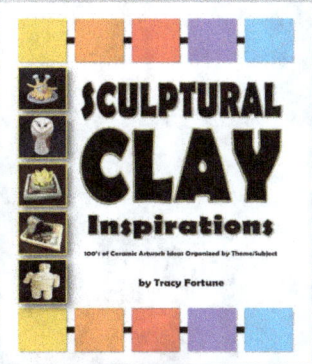 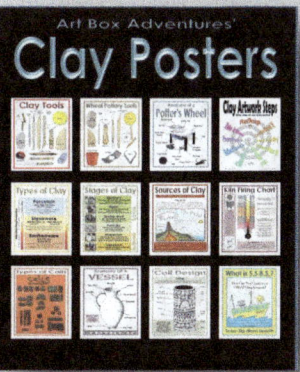

www.artboxadventures.net

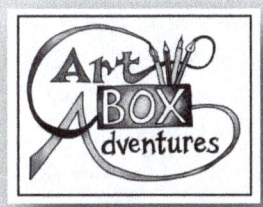  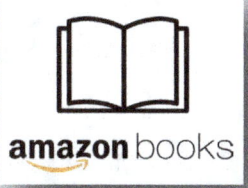

Website   Digital Downloads   Paperback Books

Contents Index

1. **Introduction** 4
   - Letter from the Author
   - How Do You Say 'Clay'?
   - Comparing Clay, Ceramics & Pottery

2. **Attributes of Clay & Glaze** 7
   - What is Clay?
   - Types of Clay
   - Sources of Clay
   - Properties of Clay
   - Clay Chemistry
   - Stages of Clay
   - The Ceramic Process
   - What is Glaze?
   - Properties of Glaze
   - Glaze Chemistry

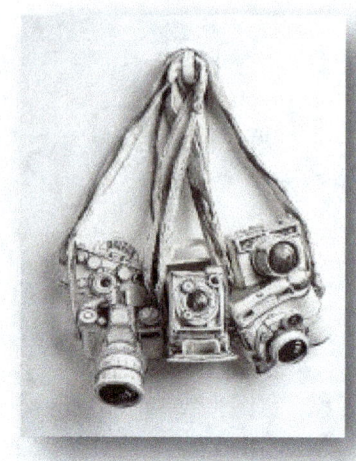

3. **Tools and Equipment** 18
   - Clay Tools
   - Clay Equipment
   - Slab Making Tools
     ◊ Tools for Creating Slabs
     ◊ Anatomy of a Slab Roller
     ◊ Tips for Using a Slab Roller
   - Extruders
     ◊ Types of Extruders
     ◊ Anatomy of a Handheld Extruder
     ◊ Anatomy of a Wall Extruder
     ◊ How to Use an Extruder
   - Potter's Wheel
     ◊ Anatomy of a Pottery Wheel
     ◊ Wheel Pottery Tools
     ◊ Tips for the Potter's Wheel
   - Pug Mill
     ◊ Anatomy of a Pug Mill
     ◊ How to Use a Pug Mill
   - Kiln
     ◊ Anatomy of a Kiln
     ◊ Types of Kilns
     ◊ Kiln Loading Tips
     ◊ Kiln Firing Chart

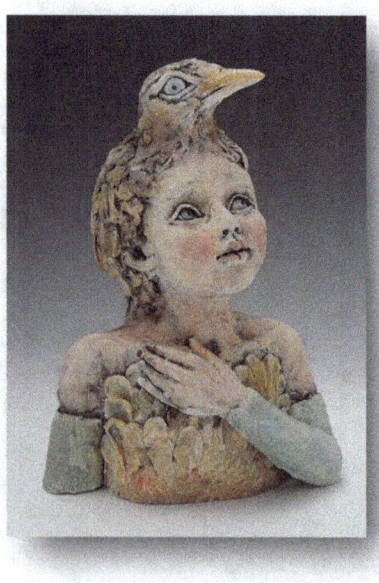
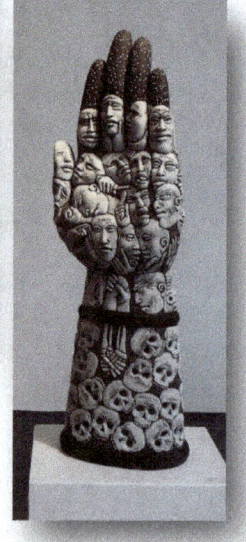

www.artboxadventures.net   artboxadventures@gmail.com

Contents Index
Continued

4. **Clay Methods Vocabulary**..................39
   - Wedging Clay Terms
   - Clay Forming Methods
   - Wheel Throwing Terms
   - Pinch Pot Terms
   - Coiling Terms
   - Types of Coils
   - Slab Method Terms
   - Extruding Terms
   - Slump & Drape Mold Terms
   - Modeling/Sculpting Terms
   - Slip Casting Terms
   - Surface Decoration Terms
   - Finishing Methods Terms

5. **Sculptural & Functional Vocab**.........53
   - Form and Function Terms
   - Clay Sculpture Types
   - Relief Sculpture Terms
   - What is a Vessel?
   - Anatomy of a Vessel
   - Geometric Vessel Forms
   - Curved Geometric Forms

6. **Elements & Principles**...................61
   - Element of Design for Clay Sculpture
     - Line
     - Shape
     - Form
     - Space
     - Volume and Mass
     - Color
     - Texture
     - Value
   - Principles of Design for Clay Sculpture
     - Balance
     - Contrast
     - Emphasis
     - Proportion & Scale
     - Repetition & Pattern
     - Rhythm & Movement
     - Unity
     - Variety
   - Surface Design Terms

7. **Ceramics Studio Tips**.....................81

8. **Glossary of Ceramic Terms**..............87
   - Glossary of Ceramic Terms

9. **Content Index**.............................98

www.artboxadventures.net   artboxadventures@gmail.com

Thank You to Consultant/Editors

Rhonda Nowak

Cora Cummins

Shannon Leenstra-Fike

Wendie Love

Stephanie Massey

Tim McAuliffe

Lela Pohlmann

Alison Thompson

Alisia Cannon

Danielle Sampognaro

SPEAKING OF CLAY

A Vocabulary Resource for Ceramics Teachers and Students

By Tracy Fortune

National Board Certified Art Teacher

Bachelor of Education, Masters of Education

Copyright © Tracy Fortune 2021

First Edition

artboxadventures@gmail.com

www.artboxadventures.net